MASTERING THE
CAEL!

2 Full-Length Practice Tests, Tutorials and Proven Strategies

Complete Test Preparation Inc.
WWW.TEST-PREPARATION.CA

Copyright 2025 Complete Test Preparation Inc.   All Rights Reserved.

No part of this book may be reproduced or transferred in any form or by any means, graphic, electronic, or mechanical, including photocopying, recording, web distribution, taping, or by any information storage retrieval system, without the written permission of the author.

Notice: Complete Test Preparation Inc. makes every reasonable effort to obtain from reliable sources accurate, complete, and timely information about the tests covered in this book. Nevertheless, changes can be made in the tests or the administration of the tests at any time and Complete Test Preparation Inc. makes no representation or warranty, either expressed or implied as to the accuracy, timeliness, or completeness of the information contained in this book. Complete Test Preparation Inc. make no representations or warranties of any kind, express or implied, about the completeness, accuracy, reliability, suitability or availability with respect to the information contained in this document for any purpose. Any reliance you place on such information is therefore strictly at your own risk.

The author(s) shall not be liable for any loss incurred as a consequence of the use and application, directly or indirectly, of any information presented in this work. Sold with the understanding, the author is not engaged in rendering professional services or advice. If advice or expert assistance is required, the services of a competent professional should be sought.

The company, product and service names used in this publication are for identification purposes only. All trademarks and registered trademarks are the property of their respective owners. Complete Test Preparation Inc. is not affiliated with any educational institution.

We strongly recommend that students check with exam providers for up-to-date information regarding test content.

CAEL® is a registered trademark of Paragon Testing Enterprises who are not involved in the production of, and do not endorse this publication.

Questions are provided for skill practice only.

ISBN-13: 9781772455328

Version 9 January 2025

About Complete Test Preparation Inc.

Why Us?
The Complete Test Preparation Team has been publishing high quality study materials since 2005, with a catalogue of over 145 titles, in English, French and Chinese, as well as ESL curriculum for all levels.

To keep up with the industry changes, we update everything all the time!

And the best part?
With every purchase, you're helping people all over the world improve themselves and their education. So thank you in advance for supporting this mission with us! Together, we are truly making a difference in the lives of those often forgotten by the system.

Charities that we support
https://www.test-preparation.ca/charities-and-non-profits/

You have definitely come to the right place.
If you want to spend your valuable study time where it will help you the most - we've got you covered today and tomorrow.

Published by
Complete Test Preparation Inc.
Victoria BC Canada

Visit us on the web at https://www.test-preparation.ca
Printed in the USA

Feedback

We welcome your feedback. Email us at feedback@test-preparation.ca with your comments and suggestions. We carefully review all suggestions and often incorporate reader suggestions into upcoming versions. As a Print on Demand Publisher, we update our products frequently.

Contents

8 Getting Started
How this study guide is organized	9
The CAEL® Study Plan	9
Making a Study Schedule	12
Getting the Most from Practice Questions	14
After Completing a Practice Test	15

18 Listening
Listening Self-Assessment	21
Answer Key	30
Listening Tips and Tricks	32

34 Reading Comprehension
Reading Comprehension Self Assessment	35
Answer Key	47
Help with Reading Comprehension	49

53 Writing
Part 1 - Write an Email	53
Sample Email 1	54
Sample Email 2	55
Responding to a Survey	56
Making Arguments To Support Your Claim	57
Organizing Your Ideas Effectively	58
Sample Essay 1 Opinion	61
Sample Essay 2: Problem-Solution	62
Common Essay Mistakes - Example 1	64
Common Essay Mistakes - Example 2	66
Writing Concisely	69
Avoiding Redundancy	71

62 Speaking
The CAEL® Speaking Questions	78
Speaking Review and Examples	79
Speaking - Example 2	80
Speaking - Giving Advice - Example 1	81
Speaking Giving Advice - Example 2	82
Speaking - Example 1	83
Speaking - Example 2	85
Comparing and Persuading - Example 1	86
Comparing and Persuading - Example 2	87

	Persuade your Friend to Choose - 1	88
	Persuade your Friend to Choose - 2	90
	Dealing with a Difficult Situation - 1	91
	Dealing with a difficult situation - 2	92

94 Practice Test Questions Set 1
  Answer Key — 122
  Analyzing your practice tests — 128

129 Practice Test Questions Set 2
  Answer Key — 159

167 How to Prepare for a Test
  The Strategy of Studying — 169

171 How to Take a Test
  Reading the Instructions — 171
  How to Take a Test - The Basics — 172
  In the Test Room – What you MUST do! — 176
  Avoid Anxiety Before a Test — 181
  Common Test-Taking Mistakes — 183

185 Conclusion

186 Online Resources

Getting Started

CONGRATULATIONS! By deciding to take the Canadian Academic English Language Assessment® (CAEL®), you have taken the first step toward a great future! Of course, there is no point in taking this important examination unless you intend to do your best to earn the highest grade you possibly can. That means getting yourself organized and discovering the best approaches, methods and strategies to master the material. Yes, that will require real effort and dedication on your part, but if you are willing to focus your energy and devote the study time necessary, before you know it you will be opening that letter of acceptance to the school of your dreams.

We know that taking on a new endeavour can be scary, and it is easy to feel unsure of where to begin. That's where we come in. This study guide is designed to help you improve your test-taking skills, show you a few tricks of the trade and increase both your competency and confidence.

The Canadian Academic English Language Assessment®

The CAEL® exam is composed of three sections, Speaking, Integrated Reading, Integrated listening, with 2 optional sections, Academic Unit A, and Academic B.

While we seek to make our guide as comprehensive as possible, note that like all exams, the CAEL® might be adjusted at some future point. New material might be added, or content that is no longer relevant or applicable might be removed. It is always a good idea to give the materials you receive when you register to take the CAEL® a careful review.

How this study guide is organized

This study guide is divided into three sections. The first section, self-assessments, which will help you recognize your areas of strength and weaknesses. This will be a boon when it comes to managing your study time most efficiently; there is not much point of focusing on material you have already got firmly under control. Instead, taking the self-assessments will show you where that time could be much better spent. In this area you will begin with a few questions to evaluate quickly your understanding of material that is likely to appear on the CAEL®. If you do poorly in certain areas, simply work carefully through those sections in the tutorials and then try the self-assessment again.

The second section, tutorials, offers information in each of the content areas, as well as strategies to help you master that material. The tutorials are not intended to be a complete course, but cover general principles. If you find that you do not understand the tutorials, it is recommended that you seek out additional instruction.

Third, we offer two sets of practice test questions, similar to those on the CAEL® Exam.

The CAEL® Study Plan

Now that you have made the decision to take the CAEL®, it is time to get started. Before you do another thing, you will need to figure out a plan of attack. The very best study tip is to start early! The longer the time period you devote to regular study practice, the more likely you will be to retain the material and be able to access it quickly. If you thought that 1x20 is the same as 2x10, guess what? It really is not, when it comes to study time. Reviewing material for just an hour per day over the course of 20 days is far better than studying for two hours a day for only 10 days. The more often you revisit a particular piece of information, the better you will know it. Not only will your grasp and understanding be better, but your ability to reach into your brain and quickly and efficiently pull out the tidbit you need, will be greatly enhanced as well.

The great Chinese scholar and philosopher Confucius believed that true knowledge could be defined as knowing what you know and what you do not know. The first step in preparing for the CAEL® Exam is to assess your strengths and weaknesses. You may already have an idea of what you know and what you do not know, but evaluating yourself using our Self- Assessment modules for each of the three areas, Speaking, Reading and Listening, will clarify the details.

Making a Study Schedule

To make your study time the most productive, you will need to develop a study plan. The purpose of the plan is to organize all the bits of pieces of information in such a way that you will not feel overwhelmed. Rome was not built in a day, and learning everything you will need to know to pass the CAEL® Exam is going to take time, too. Arranging the material you need to learn into manageable chunks is the best way to go. Each study session should make you feel as though you have accomplished your goal, or at least are a little closer, and your goal is simply to learn what you planned to learn during that particular session. Try to organize the content in such a way that each study session builds upon previous ones. That way, you will retain the information, be better able to access it, and review the previous bits and pieces at the same time.

Self-assessment

The Best Study Tip! The very best study tip is to start early! The longer you study regularly, the more you will retain and 'learn' the material. Studying for 1 hour per day for 20 days is far better than studying for 2 hours for 10 days.

What don't you know?

The first step is to assess your strengths and weaknesses. You may already have an idea of where your weaknesses are, or you can take our Self-assessment modules for each of the areas, Math, English (Optional) and Reading Comprehension (Optional).

Exam Component	Rate 1 to 5
Listening	
Problem Solving	
Daily Life Conversations	
News Items	
Discussions	
Viewpoints	
Reading	
Correspondence	
Diagrams	
Information	
Viewpoints	
Writing	
Writing an Email	
Survey Questions	
Speaking	
Giving Advice	
Personal Experiences	
Describing a scene	
Making Predictions	
Comparing and Persuading	
Difficult Situations	
Expressing Opinions	

Making a Study Schedule

The key to making a study plan is to divide the material you need to learn into manageable size and learn it, while at the same time reviewing the material that you already know.

Using the table above, any scores of 3 or below, you need to spend time learning, going over and practicing this subject area. A score of 4 means you need to review the material, but you don't have to spend time re-learning. A score of 5 and you are OK with just an occasional review before the exam.

A score of 0 or 1 means you really need to work on this area and should allocate the most time and the highest priority. Some students prefer a 5-day plan and others a 10-day plan. It also depends on how much time until the exam.

Here is an example of a 5-day plan based on an example from the table above:

Daily Conversations: 1 Study 1 hour everyday – review on last day
Listening to News: 3 Study 1 hour for 2 days then ½ hour a day, then review
Reading Comprehension: 4 Review every second day
Reading Viewpoints: 2 Study 1 hour on the first day – then ½ hour everyday
Giving Advice: 5 Review for ½ hour every other day
Making Predictions: 5 very confident – review a few times.

Using this example, Giving Advice and Making Predictions are good, and only need occasional review. Listening to News is also good and needs 'some' review. Making Predictions need a bit of work, Reading Viewpoints need a lot of work and Daily Conversations are very weak and need the majority of time. Based on this, here is a sample study plan:

Day	Subject	Time
Monday		
Study	Daily Conversations	1 hour
Study	Reading Viewpoints	1 hour
	½ **hour break**	
Study	Listening to News	1 hour
Review	Making Predictions	½ hour
Tuesday		
Study	Daily Conversations	1 hour
Study	Reading Viewpoints	½ hour
	½ **hour break**	
Study	Making Predictions	½ hour
Review	Reading Comprehension	½ hour
Review	Making Predictions	½ hour
Wednesday		
Study	Daily Conversations	1 hour
Study	Reading Viewpoints	½ hour
	½ **hour break**	
Study	Listening to News	½ hour
Review	Making Predictions	½ hour
Thursday		
Study	Daily Conversations	½ hour
Study	Reading Viewpoints	½ hour
Review	Listening to News	½ hour
	½ **hour break**	
Review	Making Predictions	½ hour
Review	Reading Comprehension	½ hour

Friday		
Review	Daily Conversations	½ hour
Review	Reading Viewpoints	½ hour
Review	Listening to News	½ hour
	½ hour break	
Review	Reading Comprehension	½ hour
Review	Making Predictions	½ hour

Getting the Most from Practice Questions

Taking a practice test is probably the best way to prepare for a test.

Quick tips to get the most from practice questions:

Simulate Test Conditions

- Choose a quiet, distraction-free environment.

- Use a timer and allow just under 1 minute per question.

- Avoid using notes or online texts

Take it seriously -

- Treat the practice test as if it's the real exam -

- Familiarize yourself with the format and topics - this will reduce anxiety.

After Completing a Practice Test

Reviewing your work after you take a practice test is critical.

Immediate Review

- Make a note of any questions you found challenging or topics that felt unfamiliar or difficult.

- How was your time management?

- Overall comfort during the test?

Do a Thorough Review

- Go over your answers focusing on correct and incorrect answers.

- For incorrect answers, identify misunderstandings knowledge gaps or problem subject areas - here is where you need to spend your study time.

Look for Patterns

- Look for recurring themes in your errors to pinpoint specific areas needing improvement.

- Assess whether mistakes were due to content gaps, misinterpretation of questions, or time constraints.

Make a Study Plan and Schedule

Complete Guide to Making a Study Plan
https://test-preparation.ca/how-to-make-a-study-plan/

How to Take a Computerized Test

Hey there! Getting ready for your computerized test? Don't worry; we've got you covered! Computerized tests, or CBEs (Computer-Based Exams), are becoming super common and have some neat advantages over the traditional pencil-and-paper style. Let's dive into what you need to know!

What are Computer-Based Exams?

CBEs are digital assessments that can evaluate all sorts of subjects—from psychometrics to health knowledge. They can be taken from anywhere, whether it's your comfy couch at home or a computer lab at your college, which is pretty cool! Plus, they give you instant feedback on your score, saving time for both you and your teachers.

Tips for Success on a Computerized Test

1. Study Hard!
This might seem obvious, but knowing your stuff is key! Good study habits will help you ace that test, no matter the format. Know your stuff!

2. Get Familiar with the Platform
Don't wait until test day to try out the software! Practice using the platform so you feel comfortable navigating it. Many computerized tests have practice tests online—use them!

3. Use Tutorials
Check out video tutorials specifically designed for your test. They explain step-by-step how to use the system and can really help calm those pre-exam nerves.

Make a note of subjects or sections that you don't understand and concentrate your study time there.

4. Arrive Early
Good advice for any test - Always get there early! This gives you a chance to settle in, relax, and get familiar with your surroundings before the test begins.

5. Ask Questions
If something isn't clear, don't hesitate to ask! Your teachers are there to help you, and your question might just help someone else too.

6. Use the Scratch Paper Provided
Use scratch paper to jot down notes, calculations, or anything that helps you think through the questions.

7. Focus on Your Answers, Not the Algorithm
The questions will be given to you in a certain order and the level of difficulty will vary depending on your answers. Don't waste your brainpower trying to figure out how the test works. Focus on answering the questions to the best of your ability!

8. Keep an Eye on the Time
Stay aware of how much time you have left, and don't get too stuck on one question. If you're unsure, skip it and move on! Don't speed through but don't hang around either.

You got this!
Remember, computerized tests are just another tool to assess your knowledge. With the right preparation and attitude, you'll do great. So, get organized, stay calm, and good luck with your exam!

Listening

THIS SECTION CONTAINS A SELF-ASSESSMENT AND LISTENING COMPREHENSION TUTORIALS. The Tutorials are designed to familiarize general principles and the Self-Assessment contains general questions similar to the questions likely to be on the CAEL®, but are not intended to be identical to the exam questions and the questions here are for skill practice only. The tutorials are not designed to be a complete course, and it is assumed that you have some familiarity with listening comprehension. If you do not understand parts of the tutorial, or find the tutorial difficult, it is recommended that you seek out additional instruction.

The purpose of the self-assessment is:

- Identify your strengths and weaknesses.

- Develop your personalized study plan (above)

- Get accustomed to the CAEL® format

- Extra practice – the self-assessments are almost a full 3rd practice test!

Since this is a Self-assessment, and depending on how confident you are with listening comprehension, timing is optional. The CAEL® has about 40 listening comprehension questions to be answered in 50 minutes. The self-assessment has 20 questions, so allow about 25 minutes to complete this assessment.

The listening section of the CAEL® includes questions on, solving a problem, daily conversations, listening for information, listening to news, listening to discussions, and listening to different viewpoints.

The questions below are not the same as you will find on the CAEL® - that would be too easy! And nobody knows what the questions will be and they change all the time. Below are general listening comprehension questions that cover the same areas as the CAEL®. So, while the format and exact wording of the questions may differ slightly, and change from year to year, if you can answer the questions below, you will have no problem with the listening comprehension section of the CAEL®.

The self-assessment is designed to give you a baseline score in the different areas covered. Here is a brief outline of how your score on the self-assessment relates to your understanding of the material.

75% - 100%	Excellent – you have mastered the content
50 – 75%	Good. You have a working knowledge. Even though you can just pass this section, you may want to review the Tutorials and do some extra practice to see if you can improve your mark.
25% - 50%	Below Average. You do not understand listening comprehension problems. Review the tutorials, and retake this quiz again in a few days, before proceeding to the rest of the practice test questions.
Less than 25%	Poor. You have a very limited understanding of listening comprehension problems. Please review the tutorials, and retake this quiz again in a few days, before proceeding to the rest of the practice test questions.

After taking the Self-Assessment, use the table above to assess your understanding. If you scored low, read through the Tutorial, Help with leading comprehension

What is a QR Code? A QR code looks like a barcode and it's used as a shortcut to link to content online using your phone's camera, saving you from typing lengthy addresses into your mobile browser.

Note: If you have difficulty with multiple QR codes on a page, cover all codes except the one you want.

Self-Assessment Answer Sheet

	A	B	C	D
1	○	○	○	○
2	○	○	○	○
3	○	○	○	○
4	○	○	○	○
5	○	○	○	○
6	○	○	○	○
7	○	○	○	○
8	○	○	○	○
9	○	○	○	○
10	○	○	○	○
11	○	○	○	○
12	○	○	○	○
13	○	○	○	○
14	○	○	○	○
15	○	○	○	○
16	○	○	○	○
17	○	○	○	○
18	○	○	○	○
19	○	○	○	○
20	○	○	○	○

Section 1 - Problem Solving

Directions: Scan the QR codes or enter the URL into your browser to hear the audio.

You will hear a short passage. Next you will hear 3 questions. You have 15 seconds to answer each question. Choose the best choice for your answer.

Passage 1 - On the Bus - Questions 1 - 3

Passage Only

Passage and Questions

1.

      a. Because she likes hockey
      b. Because her cousin is playing
      c. She goes to every game
      d. None of the above

2.

      a. Yes, she goes all the time because she knows where it is.
      b. She only goes occasionally
      c. No, she hasn't gone before because she doesn't know where it is.
      d. None of the above.

3.
   a. The street sign for Fort street.
   b. The bus sign for the number 715
   c. The address sign of her
   cousins's house
   d. None of the above

Passage 1 - On the Bus - Part II - Questions 4 - 6

Passage Only

Passage and Questions

4.
   a. She was going to the party at her home
   b. She was going home
   c. She was going to her cousin's house for a party
   d. None of the above

5.
   a. She had to walk about 5 - 10 minutes
   b. She had to walk about 15 - 20 minutes
   c. She had to walk about 20 - 30 minutes
   d. None of the above

6.
   a. The bus driver wished her good night
   b. The bus driver wished her to have a good time at the party.
   c. The bus driver wished her a good rest
   d. None of the above

Passage 1 - On the Bus - Part III - Questions 7 - 8

Passage Only

Passage and Questions

7.

    a. She said he was a good player
    b. She said he was a nice young guy
    c. She didn't say anything about him
    d. None of the above

8.

    a. He said her day was more fun than his
    b. He said he had a bad day
    c. He didn't say anything about his day
    d. None of the above

Section II - Everyday Conversations

Conversation I - Questions 9 - 11

Passage Only

Passage and Questions

9.

    a. She couldn't finish the project
    b. The project had to be changed.
    c. She had to visit their son's school
    d. None of the above.

10.

    a. Meet with the teacher
    b. Hire a tutor
    c. He would tutor their son after dinner
    d. None of the above

11.

    a. It was cancelled.
    b. They have to make big changes
    to the next part.
    c. Nothing in particular.
    d. None of the above.

Section III - Reading for Information

Passage I - Caterpillar - Questions 12 - 15

Passage Only

Passage and Questions

12.

    a. Eating

    b. Sleeping

    c. Communicating with ants.

    d. None of the above

13.

    a. Yes

    b. No, some eat insects

14.

    a. They do not receive any benefit.

    b. Ants give them protection.

    c. Ants give them food.

    d. Ants give them honeydew secretions.

15.

    a. Ants benefit most
    b. Larvae benefit most
    c. Both benefit about the same
    d. Neither benefits

Section IV - News Story

News Story I - Questions 16 - 18

Passage Only

Passage and Questions

16.
    a. At home
    b. Visiting their friend upstairs
    c. Downtown for the day
    d. In the backyard

17.
    a. Candles left burning near some papers
    b. We don't know the cause
    c. The flames started from cooking breakfast
    d. The upstairs neighbor

18.

    a. Yes
    b. No
    c. We cannot tell from the story

Section V - Point of View

Passage 1 - Native Land Claims - Questions 19 - 20

Passage Only

Passage and Questions

19.

    a. As a way to legalize ownership of land for settlement by Europeans
    b. To provide land to First Nations
    c. To give up their status as sovereign nations
    d. None of the above.

20.

    a. As a way to legalize ownership of land for settlement by Europeans
    b. To give settlers the right to use the land for farming.
    c. To transfer ownership of the land
    d. None of the above

Answer Key

1. B
She is going to the game because her cousin is playing.

2. C
She has not been before because she doesn't know how to get there.

3. B
On the way back, the driver tells her to look for the bus sign for the number 715.

4. C
After the game, she was going to her cousin's house for a party.

5. B
After getting off the bus, she had to walk 15 - 20 minutes.

6. B
The bus driver wished her a good time at the party

7. B
She said he was a nice young guy.

8. A
He said that her day was more fun than his day.

9. C
She had a bad day because she had to visit their son's school.

10. B
They decided to hire a tutor to help their son with math.

11. B
His project has major changes going forward.

12. A
Caterpillars spend most of their time eating.

Listening

13. B
Some caterpillars are herbivores, others eat other insects (carnivores).

14. B
From the passage, the ants provide some degree of protection.

15. C
The association is mutual so they both benefit.

16. C
The owners, Mary and John Smith went downtown for the day.

17. A
A candle was left burning near some papers on a bookshelf is the correct answer.

18. A
Yes their home burned down completely.

19. A
The Government of Canada saw treaties as a way to legalize ownership of land for settlement by Europeans.

20. B
To give settlers the right to use the land for farming.

Listening Tips and Tricks

Listening Comprehension tests are a kind of standardized evaluations that have a spoken passage or conversation, followed by multiple-choice questions from the passage.

Tips to get through a Listening Comprehension Exam

1. Engage in Active Listening Practice

Regularly listen to English-language materials such as podcasts, news broadcasts, academic lectures, and audiobooks. This will help you become familiar with different accents, speech patterns, and academic vocabulary, improving your overall comprehension skills.

2. Expand Your Vocabulary Systematically

Building a bigger vocabulary is crucial for understanding spoken content. Maintain a personal word list or dictionary by noting new words and phrases, reviewing them regularly, and incorporating them into your daily language use.

3. Develop Effective Note-Taking Skills

During the listening section, quick notes will help you remember key information. Use abbreviations, symbols, and shorthand to quickly jot down main ideas, supporting details, and specific data. How to take notes -

https://test-preparation.ca/taking-power-notes/

4. Familiarize Yourself with Question Types

Understanding the question types and formats—such as multiple-choice, note completion, and summarizing information—will help you develop your listening strategy.

5. Focus on Main Ideas and Supporting Details

Train yourself to identify the central themes and supporting points in spoken passages. Don't let other information distract.

6. Practice Predicting Content

Practice predicting the direction of a discussion or lecture based on the introduction, or clues in the context. This will keeps you actively engaged and prepares you for the information and questions coming next.

7. Simulate Test Conditions

Simulate a real test with practice questions. Time yourself and wear headphones.

8. Review and Analyze your Mistakes

Good advice for any test. After completing practice questions, review your responses to understand any errors.

9. Seek Constructive Feedback

Talk to instructors, tutors, or study partners. Listen and give constructive criticism into strengths and weaknesses, guiding

10. Practice Consistently

Regular and deliberate practice is key to improvement any type of skill. Dedicate time everyday to listening to build confidence and competence.

Reading Comprehension

THIS SECTION CONTAINS A SELF-ASSESSMENT AND READING COMPREHENSION TUTORIALS. The tutorials are designed to familiarize general principles and the self-assessment contains general questions similar to the reading comprehension questions likely to be on the CAEL®, but are not intended to be identical to the exam questions, **and are intended for skill practice only**. The tutorials are not designed to be a complete reading comprehension course, and it is assumed that students have some familiarity with reading comprehension questions. If you do not understand parts of the tutorial, or find the questions or tutorials difficult, it is recommended that you seek out additional instruction.

Tour of the CAEL® Reading Comprehension Content

The CAEL® reading comprehension section has 40 reading comprehension questions. Below is a detailed list of the types of reading questions that generally appear on the CAEL®.

- Reading Correspondence
- Reading Diagrams
- Reading for Information
- Reading Viewpoints

The questions below are not the same as you will find on the CAEL® - that would be too easy! And nobody knows what the questions will be and they change all the time. Mostly the changes consist of substituting new questions for old, but the changes can be new question formats or styles, changes to the number of questions in each section, changes to the time limits for each section and combining sections. Below are general reading questions that cover the same areas as the CAEL® for skill practice. So, while the format and exact wording of the questions may differ slightly, and change from year to year, if you can answer the questions below, you will have no problem with the reading comprehension section of the CAEL®.

Reading Comprehension Self Assessment

The purpose of the self-assessment is:

- Identify your strengths and weaknesses.

- Develop your personalized study plan (above)

- Get accustomed to the CAEL® format

- Extra practice – the self-assessments are almost a full 3rd practice test!

- Provide a baseline score for preparing your study schedule.

Since this is a Self-assessment, and depending on how confident you are with Reading Comprehension, timing is optional. The CAEL® usually has about 40 reading comprehension questions. The self-assessment has 14 questions, so allow about 20 minutes to complete this assessment.

Once complete, use the table below to assess your understanding of the content, and prepare your study schedule described in chapter 1.

80% - 100%	Excellent – you have mastered the content
60 – 79%	Good. You have a working knowledge. Even though you can just pass this section, you may want to review the tutorials and do some extra practice to see if you can improve your mark.
40% - 59%	Below Average. You do not understand the reading comprehension problems. Review the tutorials , and retake this quiz again in a few days, before proceeding to the practice test questions.
Less than 40%	Poor. You have a very limited understanding of the reading comprehension problems. Please review the tutorials , and retake this quiz again in a few days, before proceeding to the practice test questions.

Reading Comprehension
Self-Assessment Answer Sheet

	A	B	C	D
1	○	○	○	○
2	○	○	○	○
3	○	○	○	○
4	○	○	○	○
5	○	○	○	○
6	○	○	○	○
7	○	○	○	○
8	○	○	○	○
9	○	○	○	○
10	○	○	○	○
11	○	○	○	○
12	○	○	○	○
13	○	○	○	○
14	○	○	○	○
15	○	○	○	○

Directions: The following questions are based on several reading passages. Each passage is followed by a series of questions. Read each passage carefully, and then answer the questions based on it. You may reread the passage as often as you wish. When you have finished answering the questions based on one passage, go right onto the next passage. Choose the best answer based on the information given.

Questions 1 - 4 refer to the following passage.

Keeping Tropical Fish

Keeping tropical fish at home or in your office used to be very popular. Today, interest has declined, but it remains as rewarding and relaxing a hobby as ever. Ask any tropical fish hobbyist, and you will hear how soothing and relaxing watching colorful fish live their lives in the aquarium. If you are considering keeping tropical fish as pets, here is a list of the basic equipment you will need.

A filter is essential for keeping your aquarium clean and your fish alive and healthy. There are different types and sizes of filters and the right size for you depends on the size of the aquarium and the level of stocking. Generally, you need a filter with a 3 to 5 times turn over rate per hour. This means that the water in the tank should go through the filter about 3 to 5 times per hour.

Most tropical fish do well in water temperatures ranging between 24^0 C and 26^0 C, though each has its own ideal water temperature. A heater with a thermostat is necessary to regulate the water temperature. Some heaters are submersible and others are not, so check carefully before you buy.

Lights are also necessary, and come in a large variety of types, strengths and sizes. A light source is necessary for plants in the tank to photosynthesize and give the tank a more attractive appearance. Even if you plan to use plastic plants, the fish still require light, although here you can use a lower strength light source.

A hood is necessary to keep dust, dirt and unwanted materials out of the tank. Sometimes the hood can also help prevent evaporation. Another requirement is aquarium gravel. This will improve the aesthetics of the aquarium and is necessary if you plan to have real plants.

1. What is the general tone of this article?

    a. Formal

    b. Informal

    c. Technical

    d. Opinion

2. What evidence does the author provide to support their claim that aquarium lights are necessary?

    a. Plants require light.

    b. Fish and plants require light.

    c. The author does not provide evidence for this statement.

    d. Aquarium lights make the aquarium more attractive.

3. Which of the following is an opinion?

    a. Filter with a 3 to 5 times turn over rate per hour are required.

    b. Aquarium gravel improves the aesthetics of the aquarium.

    c. An aquarium hood keeps dust, dirt and unwanted materials out of the tank.

    d. Each type of tropical fish has its own ideal water temperature.

4. Is keeping tropical fish popular today?

    a. Yes keeping tropical fish is a popular hobby.

    b. No interest in keeping tropical fish has declined.

    c. Yes keeping tropical fish is more popular than ever.

    d. None of the above

Questions 5 - 8 refer to the following passage.

The Civil War

The Civil War began on April 12, 1861. The first shots of the Civil War were fired in Fort Sumter, South Carolina. Note that even though more American lives were lost in the Civil War than in any other war, not one person died on that first day. The war began because eleven Southern states seceded from the Union and tried to start their own government, The Confederate States of America.

Why did the states secede? The issue of slavery was a primary cause of the Civil War. The eleven southern states relied heavily on their slaves to foster their farming and plantation lifestyles. The northern states, many of whom had already abolished slavery, did not feel that the southern states should have slaves. The north wanted to free all the slaves and President Lincoln's goal was to both end slavery and preserve the Union. He had Congress declare war on the Confederacy on April 14, 1862. For four long, blood soaked years, the North and South fought.

From 1861 to mid 1863, it seemed as if the South would win this war. However, on July 1, 1863, an epic three day battle was waged on a field in Gettysburg, Pennsylvania. Gettysburg is remembered for being the bloodiest battle in American history. At the end of the three days, the North turned the tide of the war in their favor. The North then went on to dominate the South for the remainder of the war. Most well remembered might be General Sherman's "March to The Sea," where he famously led the Union Army through Georgia and the Carolinas, burning and destroying everything in their path.

In 1865, the Union army invaded and captured the Confederate capital of Richmond Virginia. Robert E. Lee, leader of the Confederacy surrendered to General Ulysses S. Grant, leader of the Union forces, on April 9, 1865. The Civil War was over and the Union was preserved.

5. Which of the following statements summarizes a FACT from the passage?

    a. Congress declared war and then the Battle of Fort Sumter began.

    b. Congress declared war after shots were fired at Fort Sumter.

    c. President Lincoln was pro slavery

    d. President Lincoln was at Fort Sumter with Congress

6. Which event finally led the Confederacy to surrender?

    a. The battle of Gettysburg

    b. The battle of Bull Run

    c. The invasion of the confederate capital of Richmond

    d. Sherman's March to the Sea

7. What year did the Civil War begin?

    a. The Civil War began in 1861

    b. The Civil War began in 1863

    c. The Civil War began in 1862

    d. None of the Above

8. How many people died on the first day?

   a. Nobody was killed on the first day.
   b. Many people died on the first day.
   c. It is not known how many people died on the first day.
   d. None of the above.

Questions 9 - 10 refer to the following passage.

Vice President Johnson, Mr. Speaker, Mr. Chief Justice, President Eisenhower, Vice President Nixon, President Truman, reverend clergy, fellow citizens:

We observe today not a victory of party, but a celebration of freedom -- symbolizing an end, as well as a beginning -- signifying renewal, as well as change. For I have sworn before you and Almighty God the same solemn oath our forebears prescribed nearly a century and three-quarters ago.

The world is very different now. For man holds in his mortal hands the power to abolish all forms of human poverty and all forms of human life. And yet the same revolutionary beliefs for which our forebears fought are still at issue around the globe -- the belief that the rights of man come not from the generosity of the state, but from the hand of God.

We dare not forget today that we are the heirs of that first revolution. Let the word go forth from this time and place, to friend and foe alike, that the torch has been passed to a new generation of Americans -- born in this century, tempered by war, disciplined by a hard and bitter peace, proud of our ancient heritage, and unwilling to witness or permit the slow undoing of those human rights to which this nation has always been committed, and to which we are committed today at home and around the world.

Let every nation know, whether it wishes us well or ill, that we shall pay any price, bear any burden, meet any hardship, support any friend, oppose any foe, to assure the survival and the success of liberty.

Reading   43

This much we pledge -- and more.

John F. Kennedy Inaugural Address delivered 20 January 1961

9. What is the tone of this speech?

    a. Triumphant
    b. Optimistic
    c. Threatening
    d. Gloating

10. Which of the following is an opinion?

    a. The world is very different now.

    b. For man holds in his mortal hands the power to abolish all forms of human poverty and all forms of human life.

    c. We dare not forget today that we are the heirs of that first revolution

    d. For I have sworn before you and Almighty God the same solemn oath our forebears prescribed nearly a century and three-quarters ago.

Here is an online comment. Answer the questions to fill in the blanks. Questions 11 - 13.

I like the speech, as a triumphant and   [11]   speech, but I think he is being a little over-dramatic.   Ok he wants to celebrate, but it seems to me it is   [12]   ! Where are the details? Where is the plan?

I think that he should talk more about   [13]   .

11.

      a. Optimistic
      b. Pessimistic
      c. Depressing
      d. None of the above

12.

      a. All talk and no action
      b. All action and no talk
      c. Lots of plans but no action
      d. None of the above

13.

      a. The election
      b. What he is going to do
      c. What his opponents think
      d. None of the above

Getting a dog. Questions 13 - 15

Directions: Review the pictures and information below then answer the questions.

Breed: Spaniel Small dog, (40 cm.) with long hair, very smart, can be barky, needs moderate exercise	**Breed:** Golden Labrador large dog with short hair, very smart and affectionate, needs a lot of exercise

Hi Susan - hope you and Peter are good and had a great weekend. We are thinking of getting a dog and I have ____ 13 ____ to two choices. What do you think?

A lab would be great and I love them but they need ____14____ of exercise. I like the spaniels too, but they are quite ____15____.

13.

    a. Widened the choices
    b. Eliminated choices
    c. Narrowed the choices
    d. None of the above

14.

    a. A lot of food
    b. A lot of exercise
    c. A little exercise
    d. None of the above

15.

    a. Small
    b. Large
    c. bad tempered
    d. None of the above

Answer Key

1. B
The general tone is informal.

2. C
The author does not provide evidence for this statement.

3. B
The following statement is an opinion, " Aquarium gravel improves the aesthetics of the aquarium."

4. B
Interest in keeping tropical fish has declined.

5. B
Look at the dates in the passage. The shots were fired on April 12 and Congress declared war on April 14.

Choice C is incorrect because the passage states that Lincoln was against slavery. Choice D is incorrect because it never mentions who was or was not at Fort Sumter.

6. C
The passage states that Lee surrendered to Grant after the capture of the capital of the Confederacy, which is Richmond.

Choice A is incorrect because the war continued for 2 years after Gettysburg. Choice B is incorrect because that battle is not mentioned in the passage. Choice D is incorrect because the capture of the capital occurred after the march to the sea.

7. A
The Civil War began on April 12, 1861.

8. A
Nobody died on the first day.

9. A
This is a triumphant speech where President Kennedy is celebrating his victory.

10. C
The statement, "We dare not forget today that we are the heirs of that first revolution" is an opinion.

11. A
The speech is optimistic.

12. A
She feels the speech is all talk and no action.

13. B
This person feels he should talk more about what he is going to do.

14. B
Labrador require a lot of exercise.

15. A
Spaniels are quite small.

Help with Reading Comprehension

At first sight, reading comprehension tests look challenging especially if you are given long essays to answer only two to three questions. While reading, you might notice your attention waning, or feeling sleepy. Do not be discouraged because there are various tactics and long range strategies that make comprehending even long, boring essays easier.

Your friends before your foes. It is always best to start with essays or passages with familiar subjects rather than those with unfamiliar ones. This approach applies the same logic as tackling easy questions before hard ones. Skip passages that do not interest you and leave them for later.

Don't use 'special' reading techniques. This is not the time for speed-reading or anything like that – just plain ordinary reading – not too slow and not too fast.

Read through the entire passage and the questions before you do anything. Many students try reading the questions first and then looking for answers in the passage thinking this approach is more efficient. What these students do not realize is that it is often hard to navigate in unfamiliar roads. If you do not familiarize yourself with the passage first, looking for answers become not only time-consuming but also dangerous because you might miss the context of the answer you are looking for. If you read the questions first you will only confuse yourself and lose valuable time.

Familiarize yourself with reading comprehension questions. If you are familiar with the common types of reading comprehension questions, you are able to take note of important parts of the passage, saving time. There are six major kinds of reading comprehension questions.

- **Main Idea**- Questions that ask for the central thought or significance of the passage.

- **Specific Details** - Questions that asks for explicitly stated ideas.

- **Opinion and Point of View** - Questions that ask for the author's opinion or point of view.

- **Tone or Attitude** - Questions that test your ability to sense the emotional state of the author.

Read. Read. Read. The best preparation for reading comprehension tests is always to read, read and read. If you are not used to reading lengthy passages, you will probably lose concentration. Increase your attention span by making a habit out of reading.

Reading Comprehension tests become less daunting when you have trained yourself to read and understand fast. Always remember that it is easier to understand passages you are interested in. Do not read through passages hastily. Make mental notes of ideas you may be asked.

Reading Comprehension Strategy

When facing the reading comprehension section of a standardized test, you need a strategy to be successful. You want to keep several steps in mind:

- First, make a note of the time and the number of sections. Time your work accordingly. Typically, four to five minutes per section is sufficient. Second, read the directions for each selection thoroughly before beginning (and listen well to any additional verbal instructions, as they will often clarify obscure or confusing written guidelines). You must know exactly how to do what you're about to do!

- Now you're ready to begin reading the selection. Read the passage carefully, noting significant characters or events on a scratch sheet of paper or underlining on the test sheet. Many students find making a basic list in the margins helpful. Quickly jot down or underline one-word summaries of characters, notable happenings, numbers, or key ideas. This will help you better retain information and focus wandering thoughts. Remember, however, that your main goal in doing this is to find the information that answers the questions. Even if you find the passage interesting, remember your goal and work fast but stay on track.

- Now read the question and all the choices. Now you have read the passage, have a general idea of the main ideas, and have marked the important points. Read the question and all the choices. Never choose an answer without reading them all! Questions are often designed to confuse – stay focussed and clear. Usually the answer choices will focus on one or two facts or inferences from the passage. Keep these clear in your mind.

- Search for the answer. With a very general idea of what the different choices are, go back to the passage and scan for the relevant information. Watch for big words, unusual or unique words. These make your job easier as you can scan the text for the particular word.

- Mark the Answer. Now you have the key information the question is looking for. Go back to the question, quickly scan the choices and mark the correct one.

Understand and practice the different types of standardized reading comprehension tests. See the list above for the different types. Typically, there will be several questions dealing with facts from the selection, a couple more inference questions dealing with logical consequences of those facts, and periodically an application-oriented question surfaces to force you to make connections with what you already know. Some students prefer to answer the questions as listed, and feel classifying the question and then ordering is wasting precious time. Other students prefer to answer the different types of questions in order of how easy or difficult they are. The choice is yours and do whatever works for you. If you want to try answering in order of difficulty, here is a recommended order, answer fact questions first; they're easily found within the passage. Tackle inference problems next, after re-reading the question(s) as many times as you need to. Application or 'best guess' questions usually take the longest, so, save them for last.

Use the practice tests to try out both ways of answering and see what works for you.

For more help with reading comprehension, see Multiple Choice Secrets at www.multiple-choice.ca.

Reading Quick Tips

Active Reading: highlight key points, underlining or marking key information, and making marginal notes.

Preview the Questions: Before reading the passage, quickly look skim the questions to identify the information you need to focus on. This technique helps in pinpointing relevant details during your reading.

Summarize: After reading each paragraph, briefly summarize its main idea in your own words.

Watch Text Structure: Look at how the passage is organized — cause-effect, compare-contrast, or problem-solution.

Meaning in Context: If you don't recognize a word, Look for clues in the surrounding sentences to infer the meaning. Generally, you don't have to know the exact meaning.

Eliminate Wrong Answers: Elimination is the most powerful strategy for multiple-choice. Eliminating clearly wrong options improves the odds of selecting the correct answer. More on Multiple Choice Strategy here www.multiple-choice.ca

Refer Back to the Passage: Always base your answers on information directly in the text. Don't rely on prior knowledge or make assumptions

Writing

THIS SECTION CONTAINS A SELF-ASSESSMENT AND SHORT WRITING TUTORIAL. The tutorial is designed to familiarize with general principles. So, while the self-assessment contains general questions similar to the questions likely to be on the CAEL®, but are not intended to be identical to the exam questions. If you do not understand parts of the tutorial, or find the tutorial difficult, it is recommended that you seek out additional instruction.

The questions below are not the same as you will find on the CAEL® - that would be too easy! And nobody knows what the questions will be and they change all the time. Mostly the changes consist of substituting new questions for old, but the changes can be new question formats or styles, changes to the number of questions in each section, changes to the time limits for each section and combining sections. So, while the format and exact wording of the questions may differ slightly, and change from year to year, if you can answer the questions below, you will have no problem with the writing section of the CAEL®.

Part 1 - Write an Email

You recently made an online purchase and the product was not the same as the description on the website. Write a short email (150 - 200 words) that includes the following:

- What you purchased and when (for example a book)
- Exactly how it is different to the website description
- How you would like the company to fix the problem

Sample Email 1

To Whom it may concern:

> [Use 'To Whom it may concern' if you do not know the name of the manager or other responsible person.]

I recently purchased (Sept. 15) your How to Lose Weight in 30 days from your website (Receipt #12345) and I am very unhappy with my purchase.

> [This is a strong opening paragraph - date of purchase, name of product and receipt number. States that you are unhappy.]

The book, on your website, claims to have a 'complete menu planner' which I cannot find anywhere. There are many other things on your website that are missing in the book.

I think a lot of the information in your book is available for free online.

> [The second and third paragraphs explain why you are unhappy and gives an example]

I would like a refund - please let me know where to mail the book to.

> [The last paragraph asks for a refund to solve the problem.]

thank you,

Your Name

> [Ending the email is polite]

Sample Email 2

Mr. Jones:

[Address the letter to the manager or owner]

I was recently in your store (May 17 in the afternoon) and I was very unhappy with the condition of your store.

> [Opening sentence says when you were in the store and the problem]

I noticed some paper on the floor and the floor hadn't been cleaned for some time. I wanted some help finding a size and there were no staff to help me.

> [Explains more detail of the problems in the first paragraph]

I like your store, but if the store is dirty, and there are no staff to assist me, I will not buy from you.

> [Explains what you will do about the problems - go somewhere else]

I hope in the future you will be able to clean up your store and train your staff to be more helpful.

> [Polite suggestion on how to fix the problem]

thank you,

Your Name

Part II - Responding to a Survey

Writing a letter that is responding to a survey question means you will have to answer several questions:

- Which option you prefer
- Why you prefer this option
- Additional information that supports your argument

General Outline

Opening Sentence/Paragraph

State which option you prefer and a general summary of why

Second Paragraph

Details and explanation of why you prefer this option

Third/Last Paragraph

Additional information to support your argument

Example Question

Your city has funding for ONE of the following projects:

   a. Bike Lanes

   b. Renovate Recreation Center

Dear Planning Committee:

I am writing to support funding for bike lanes in or city. I feel that bike lanes are better for the environment, and a healthier choice for everyone.

If there were bike lanes I would use them frequently and so would many of my friends. I drive to work everyday and I see the road becoming more and more congested with traffic. Bike lanes would reduce the traffic congestions and pollution.

I have been to the Recreation center and do not feel that renovations are urgent or a priority.

Thank you for consideration

Your Name

Making Arguments To Support Your Claim

Have you ever won a debate or an argument? Probably. This happens all the time! Maybe you and your classmates convinced your teacher she didn't need to assign you 15 pages of homework. Or maybe you were eating out at a restaurant and it took two hours to get your food, so you talked to the manager and received a discount for your food. Or perhaps it is as simple as you and a friend are debating which movie to see and your choice is picked. How did you win these discussions? You made good arguments to support your claim.

In the Writing Section of the CAEL®, you need to make a claim and then give reasons to support your claim. This is a short tutorial on how to make an

So what is the first and most important tip to be successful in making good arguments? **Know what your claim is**!

This may sound simple but never start without knowing which side you are going to take! Surprisingly enough, don't feel like the side you argue needs to be your own personal opinion. You're not being graded on what your opinion is, but how well you support it and how well you express it! Pick the side you know the most about, and have the most evidence to support!

Next, you need to know what type of arguments will help your claim.

To break the ice let's start with an easy example. We can use the one from above when you and a friend are debating what movie to go see. The choices are How to Train Your Dragon 2 in 3D and The Edge of Tomorrow. You want to go see Edge of Tomorrow.

Select the argument that is **least** likely to get Edge of Tomorrow chosen.

> A. 3D movies are more expensive
> B. You haven't seen the first How to Train Your Dragon
> C. They both start at the same time
> D. Another friend told you Edge of Tomorrow was really good.

Hopefully you picked C. If both movies start at the same time, it is not a very good argument for your movie getting chosen. The other three, though, are valid arguments to support your claim that you and your friend should see Edge of Tomorrow.

To make solid arguments you need to:

> 1) Know what your claim is
> 2) Use fair, unbiased arguments
> 3) Ensure your evidence supports your original claim

Remember, you do this every single day! You are consistently making arguments to support your beliefs and your claims! Just apply the same logic when answering these questions!

Organizing Your Ideas Effectively

Good organization is the hardest thing to learn while writing. Here are a few tips to help you get organized and stay organized when writing.

1) Think Before You Write

Have you ever heard the saying, "Think before you speak?" Well, the same thing should happen when you are writing! Thinking your answer through before you start writing is the best way to help you stay organized. So, before you even write the first word, think through these steps.

    1) What is my purpose?
    2) What is my main idea? What side am I arguing? What am I trying to get across?
    3) What are 3-4 of the most important things I make sure I include?

Those seem like pretty easy steps, but you'll be amazed at how much they will help you stay consistent and organized in your essay.

2) Write Your Position

By thinking through steps 1 - 3 above, you probably have a pretty solid foundation to build your argument. Remember, to state your position in one sentence that clearly and concisely summarizes your main idea. It should be unbiased and leave the reader with no doubts.

3) Outline Your Paper

Now that you have your position, and have already thought through your paper, it's time to start writing. However, start by writing a brief outline of what you want to include. Now, outlines will ALL look different. Do what works for you! Some people like their outlines brief with only a main idea and 3-4 main points. Some students find it easier to add supporting evidence and information under all their main points. It doesn't matter what system you use, just make sure it works for you!

4) Write Your Paper Following Your Outline

You've thought through your paper, you have a position, and you've outlined your information. Congratulations, you are ready to start writing! Make sure you follow your outline and include all the information you wanted in step 1. In addition, make sure everything you write can be tied back to your original position!

5) Read It Out Loud (or to yourself)

Okay, so you've finished your answer and you think you're done, but there is one more crucial step at the end. Read it to yourself. This sounds foolish, but even the best writers make mistakes! It is so easy to make simple errors because you feel like you are rushed for time. Reading it to yourself will help catch almost 99% of these errors. Think about how you talk to your friends and your teachers. We typically organize our thoughts extremely well when we are speaking out loud, so when you hear your answer read back to you, you'll be able to easily catch where something doesn't sound quite right and you can fix it!

Types of Essay Prompts

Here are some sample writing prompts that reflect the types of tasks you might encounter:

Advantage/Disadvantage Essay:

Prompt: Discuss the advantages and disadvantages of implementing a four-day workweek in modern workplaces.

Opinion Essay:

Prompt: Do you agree or disagree with the statement: "Online education provides more benefits than traditional classroom education." Support your answer with reasons and examples.

Problem-Solution Essay:

Prompt: Identify a significant environmental issue affecting urban areas and propose viable solutions to address it.

Compare and Contrast Essay:

Prompt: Compare and contrast the impacts of social media on interpersonal communication in the past decade.

Argumentative Essay:

Prompt: Should governments invest more in public transportation systems to reduce traffic congestion? Present arguments for and against this proposition.

Descriptive Essay:

Prompt: Describe the key characteristics of an effective leader in today's society.

Cause and Effect Essay:

Prompt: Analyze the primary causes and effects of the increasing prevalence of remote work in recent years.

Persuasive Essay:

Prompt: Persuade your reader whether or not zoos should exist in the 21st century, providing supporting arguments.

Analytical Essay:

Prompt: Examine the role of technology in shaping modern educational practices.

Reflective Essay:

Prompt: Reflect on a personal experience that significantly influenced your academic journey and discuss its impact.

When responding to these prompts, it's essential to structure your essay clearly, develop your ideas with supporting details, and demonstrate a strong command of academic English.

Sample Essay 1 Opinion

Prompt: Do you agree or disagree with the statement: "Online education provides more benefits than traditional classroom education." Support your answer with reasons and examples.

Essay:

In recent years, online education has gained significant popularity, leading to debates about its effectiveness compared to traditional classroom education. I firmly believe that online education offers more benefits than conventional classroom settings for several reasons.

Firstly, online education provides unparalleled flexibility. Students can access course materials and lectures at their convenience, allowing them to balance studies with work or personal commitments. This flexibility is particularly advantageous for adult learners or those with irregular schedules.

Secondly, online platforms often offer a wider range of courses and programs that may not be available locally. This accessibility enables students to pursue specialized fields of interest without the need to relocate, thereby broadening their educational opportunities.

Moreover, online education fosters self-discipline and time management skills. Without the structured environment of a traditional classroom, students must take initiative and responsibility for their learning, which cultivates essential life skills applicable beyond academics.

However, it is important to acknowledge that online education may lack the immediate interpersonal interactions present in traditional classrooms. While virtual discussions and forums exist, they may not fully replicate the dynamic of face-to-face engagement.

In conclusion, despite some limitations, online education offers substantial benefits, including flexibility, accessibility, and the development of self-discipline. As technology continues to advance, it is likely that online education will play

an increasingly prominent role in the academic landscape.
Commentary:

Content and Development: The essay presents clear arguments supporting online education, with relevant examples illustrating flexibility, accessibility, and skill development.

Organization: Ideas are logically structured, with each paragraph focusing on a distinct point.

Language Use: The language is formal and appropriate for an academic context, demonstrating a good range of vocabulary and varied sentence structures.

Mechanics: The essay is free from grammatical errors and maintains proper punctuation throughout.

Sample Essay 2: Problem-Solution

Prompt: Identify a significant environmental issue affecting urban areas and propose viable solutions to address it.

Essay:

Urban areas worldwide are grappling with the pressing issue of air pollution, which poses serious health risks and environmental challenges. To mitigate this problem, several viable solutions can be implemented.

One effective approach is to enhance public transportation systems. By improving the efficiency, affordability, and coverage of buses, trains, and subways, cities can reduce the number of private vehicles on the road, thereby decreasing vehicular emissions.

Another solution involves promoting the use of renewable energy sources. Transitioning urban power grids from fossil fuels to renewable energy, such as solar or wind, can significantly lower air pollutants released from electricity generation.

Additionally, implementing green urban planning initiatives can contribute to cleaner air. Establishing green spaces, such as parks and urban forests, helps absorb pollutants and pro-

vides residents with healthier environments.
Public awareness campaigns are also crucial. Educating citizens about the sources and dangers of air pollution, as well as encouraging eco-friendly practices like carpooling and energy conservation, can foster community involvement in pollution reduction efforts.

In conclusion, addressing urban air pollution requires a multifaceted approach, including improving public transportation, adopting renewable energy, implementing green urban planning, and raising public awareness. Collaborative efforts between governments, businesses, and citizens are essential to effectively combat this environmental issue.

Commentary:

Content and Development: The essay identifies air pollution as a significant urban environmental issue and proposes clear, actionable solutions, each supported by explanation.

Organization: The response is well-organized, with each paragraph dedicated to a specific solution, enhancing readability.

Language Use: The essay employs appropriate academic language and demonstrates a variety of sentence structures, contributing to a cohesive argument.

Common Essay Mistakes - Example 1

Whether the topic is love or action, reality television shows damage society. Viewers witness the personal struggles of strangers, and they experience an outpouring of emotions in the name of entertainment. This can be dangerous on many levels. Viewers become numb to real emotions and values. Run the risk of not interpreting a dangerous situation correctly. 1 The reality show participant is also at risk because they are completely exposed. 2 The damage to both viewers and participants leads to the destruction of our healthy societal values.

Romance reality shows are dangerous to the participants and contribute to the emotional problems witnessed in society today as we set up a system built on equality and respect, shows like "The Bachelor" tear it down. 3 In front of millions of viewers every week, young women compete for a man. Twenty-five women claim to be in love with a man they just met. The man is reduced to an object they compete for. There are tears, fights, and manipulation aimed at winning the prize. 4 Imagine a young woman's reality when she returns home and faces the scrutiny of viewers who watched her unravel on television every Monday night. These women objectify themselves and have learned 5 that relationships are a combination of hysteria and competition. This does not give hope to a society based on family values and equality.

6 While incorporating the same manipulations and breakdown of relationships offered on "The Bachelor," shows like "Survivor" add another level of danger. Not only are they building a society based on lying, they are competing in physical challenges that become dangerous. In the name of entertainment, these challenges become increasingly physical and are usually held in a hostile environment. The viewer's ability to determine the safety of an activity is messed up. 7 To entertain and preserve their pride, participants continue in competitions regardless of the danger level. For example, 8 participants on "Survivor" have sustained serious injuries in as heart attack and burns. Societal rules are based on the safety of its citizens, not on hurting yourself for entertainment.

     Reality shows of all kinds are dangerous to participants. They damage society. 9

1. Correct sentence fragments. Who/what runs the risk? Add a subject or combine sentences. Try: "Viewers become numb to real emotions and run the risk of not interpreting a dangerous situation correctly."

2. Correct redundant phrases. Try: "The reality show participant is also at risk because they are exposed."

3. Correct run-on sentences. Decide which thoughts should be separated. Try: "Romance reality shows are dangerous to participants and contribute to the emotional problems of society today. As we support a system built on equality and respect, shows like "The Bachelor" tear it down."

4. Vary sentence structure and length. Try: "Twenty-five women claim to be in love with a man who is reduced to being the object of competition. There are tears, fights, and manipulation aimed at winning the prize."

5. Use active voice. Try: These women objectify themselves and learned that relationships are a combination of hysteria and competition.

6. Use transitions to tie paragraphs together. Try: Start the paragraph with, "Action oriented reality shows are equally as dangerous to the participants."

7. Avoid casual language/slang. Try: "The viewer's ability to determine the safety of an activity is compromised."

8. Don't address the essay. Avoid phrases like "for example" and "in conclusion." Try: "Participants on "Survivor" have sustained serious injuries as heart attack and burns.

9. Leave yourself time to write a strong conclusion! Try: Designate 3-5 minutes for writing your conclusion.

Common Essay Mistakes - Example 2

Questioning authority makes society stronger. In every aspect our society, there is an authoritative person or group making rules. There is also the group underneath them who are meant to follow. 1 This is true of our country's public schools as well as our federal government. The right to question authority at both levels is guaranteed by the United States Declaration of Independence. People are given the ability to question so that authority figures are kept in check 2 and will be forced to listen to the opinions of other people. Questioning authority leads to positive changes in society and preserves what is already working well.

If students never question the authority of a principal's decisions, the best interest of the student body is lost. Good things 3 may not remain in place for the students and no amendment to the rules are sought. Change requires that authority be questioned. An example is Silver Head Middle School in Davie, Florida. Last year, the principal felt strongly about enforcing the school's uniform policy. Some students were not bothered by this. 4 Many students felt the policy disregarded their civil rights. A petition voicing student dissatisfaction was signed and presented to the principal. He met with a student representative to discuss the petition. Compromise was reached as a monthly "casual day." The students were able to promote change and peace by questioning authority.

Even at the level of federal government, our country's ultimate authority, the ability to question is the key to the harmony keeping society strong. Most government officials are elected by the public so they have the right to question their authority. 5 If there's a mandate, law, or statement that citizens aren't 6 happy with, they have recourse. Campaigning for, or against a political platform and participating in the electoral process give a voice to every opinion. I think elections are very important. 7 Without this questioning and examination of society's laws, the government will represent only the voice of the authority figure. The success of our society is based on the questioning of authority. 8

Society is strengthened by those who question authority. Dialogue is created between people with different visions and change becomes possible. At both the level of public school and of federal government, the positive effects of questioning authority can be witnessed. Whether questioning the decisions of a single principal or the motives of the federal government, it is the willingness of people to question and create change that allows society to grow. A strong society is inspired by many voices, all at different levels. 9 These voices keep society strong.

1. Write concisely. Combine the sentences to improve understanding and cut unnecessary words. Try: "In every aspect of society, there is an authority making rules and a group of people meant to follow them."

2. Avoid slang. Re-word "kept in check." Try: "People are given the ability to question so that authority figures are held accountable and will be forced to listen to the opinions of other people."

2-2. Cut unnecessary words. Try: "People are given the ability to question so that authority figures are held accountable and will listen to other opinions."

3. Use precise language. What are "good things?" Try: "Interesting activities may not remain in place for the students and no amendment to the rules are sought."

Use correct subject-verb agreement. Be careful to identify the correct subject of your sentence. Try: "Interesting activities may not remain in place for the students and no amendment to the rules is sought."

4. Don't add information that doesn't add value to your argument. Cut: "Some students weren't bothered by this."

5. Check for parallel structure. Who has the right to question whose authority? Try: "Having voted them in, the people have the authority to question public officials."

6. Don't use contractions in academic essays. Try: "If there is a mandate, law, or statement that citizens are not happy with, they have recourse."

7. Don't use the pronoun "I" in persuasive essays. Cut opinions. Cut: "I think elections are very important."

8. Use specific examples to prove your argument. Try: Discuss a particular election in depth.

9. Cut redundant sentences. Cut: "A strong society is inspired by many voices, all at different levels."

Example Essay Prompts

Describe a person who has had a significant impact on your life and explain why.

Discuss the importance of teamwork in achieving success.

Analyze the effects of social media on relationships and communication.

Explain how community service can benefit individuals and society as a whole.

Compare and contrast two different cultures and discuss how they influence one another.

Describe a challenge you have faced and how you overcame it.

Discuss the impact of technology on modern education.

Explain the benefits of reading for personal growth and development.

Analyze the causes of climate change and propose potential solutions.

Reflect on a moment that changed your perspective on life.

Writing Concisely

Concise writing is direct and descriptive. The reader follows the writer's thoughts easily. If your writing is concise, a four paragraph essay is acceptable for standardized tests. It's better to write clearly about fewer ideas than to write poorly about many.

This doesn't always mean using fewer words. It means that every word you use is important to the message. Unnecessary or repetitive information dilutes ideas and weakens your writing. The meaning of the word concise comes from the Latin, "to cut up." If it isn't necessary information, don't waste precious testing minutes writing it down.

Being redundant is a quick way to lengthen a sentence or paragraph, but it takes away your power during a timed essay. While many writers use repetition of phrases and key words to make their point, it's important to remove words that don't add value. Redundancy can confuse and lead you away from your subject when you need to write quickly. Be aware that many redundant phrases are part of our daily language and need to be cut from your essay.

For example, "bouquet of flowers" is a redundant phrase as only the word "bouquet" is necessary. Its definition includes flowers. Be especially careful with words you use to stress a point, such as "completely," "totally," and "very."

First of all, I'd like to thank my family.
Revised: First, I'd like to thank my family.

The school *introduced a new* rule.
Revised: The school introduced a rule.

I am *completely full*.
Revised: I am full.

Your glass is *totally empty*!
Revised: Your glass is empty!

Her artwork is *very unique*.
Revised: Her artwork is unique.

Other ways to cut bulk and time include avoiding phrases that have no meaning or power in your essay. Phrases like "in my opinion," "as a matter of fact," and "due to the fact that" are space and time wasters. Also, change passive verbs to active voice.

In my opinion, the paper is well written.
Revised: The paper is well written.

The book *was written* by the best students.
Revised: The best students wrote the book.

The teacher *is listening* to the students.
Revised: The teacher listens to the students.
This assigns action to the subject, shortens, and clarifies the sentence. When time is working against you, precise language is on your side.

Not only should you remove redundant phrases, whole sentences without value should be cut too. Replacing general nouns with specific ones is an effective way to accomplish this.

She screamed as the thing came closer. It was a sharp-toothed dog.
Revised: She screamed as the sharp-toothed dog came closer.

The revised sentence is precise and combining sentences improves the paragraph while varying sentence structure. When editing, ask yourself which thoughts should be connected and which need to be separated. Skim each paragraph as you finish writing it and cut as you go.

Leave three to four minutes for final editing. While reading, make a point to pause at every period. This allows you to "hear" sentences the way your reader will, not how you meant them to sound. This will help you find the phrases and sentences that need to be cut or combined. The result is an essay a grader will appreciate.

Avoiding Redundancy

Duplication and verbosity in English is the use of two or more words that clearly mean the same thing, making one of them unnecessary. It is easy to do use redundant expressions or phrases in a conversation where speech is spontaneous, and common in spoken English. In written English, however, redundancy is more serious and harder to ignore. Below are a list of redundant phrases to avoid.

1. Suddenly exploded.

An explosion is instantaneous or immediate and that is sudden enough. No need to use 'suddenly' along with exploded.

2. Final outcome.

An outcome refers to the result. An outcome is intrinsically final and so no need to use final along with outcome.

3. Advance notice/planning/reservations/ warning.

A warning, notice, reservation or plan is made before an event. Once the reader sees any of these words, they know that they were done or carried out before the event. These words do not need to be used with advance.

4. First began, new beginning.

Beginning signals the start or the first time, and therefore the use of "new" is superfluous.

5. Add an additional.

The word 'add' indicates the provision of another something, and so "additional" is superfluous.

6. For a period/number of days.

The word "days" is already in plural and clearly signifies more than just one day. It is thus redundant to use "a number of," or "a period of" along with days. Simply state the number of days or of the specific number of days is unknown, you say 'many days.'

7. Foreign imports.

Imports are foreign as they come from another country, so it is superfluous to refer to imports as "foreign."

8. Forever and ever.

Forever indicates eternity and so there is no need for "ever" as it simply duplicated forever.

9. Came at a time when.

"At a time" is not necessary in this phrase because the 'when' already provides a temporal reference to the action, coming.

10. Free gift.

It cannot be a gift if it is paid for. A gift, by nature, is free and so referring to a gift is free is redundant.

11. Collaborate/join/meet/merge together.

The words merge, join, meet and collaborate already suggest people or things coming together. It is unnecessary to use any of these words with together, such as saying merge together or join together. The correct expression is to say join or merge, omitting the together.

12. Invited guests.

Guests are those invited for an event. Since they had to be invited to be guests, there is no need to use invited with guests.

13. Major breakthrough.

A breakthrough is significant by nature. It can only be described as a breakthrough when there is a notable progress. The significant nature of the progress is already implied when you use the word "breakthrough," so "major" is redundant.

14. Absolutely certain or sure/essential/ guaranteed.

When someone or something is said to be sure or certain it indicates that it is without doubt. Using "absolutely" in addition to certain, or sure, is unnecessary. Essential or guaranteed is used for something that is absolute and so also does not need the word absolutely to accompany them.

15. Ask a question.

Ask means to present a question. Using "question" and "ask" is redundant.

16. Basic fundamentals/essentials.

Using basic here is redundant. Essentials and fundamental suggest an elementary nature.

17. [Number] a.m. in the morning/p.m. in the evening.

When you write 8 a.m. the reader knows you mean 8 o'clock in the morning. It is not necessary to say 8 a.m. in the morning. Simply write 8 a.m. or 8 p.m.

18. Definite decision.

A decision is already definite even if it can be reversed later. A decision is a definite course of action has been chosen. No need to use the word definite along with the word decision.

19. Past history/record.

A record or history by definition refers to past events or occurrences. Using past to qualify history or record is unnecessary.

20. Consensus of opinion.

Consensus means agreement over something that may be or not be an opinion. So it may look that using the phrase 'consensus of opinion' is appropriate, but it is better to omit "opinion."

21. Enter in.

Enter means going in, as no one enters out. Therefore no need to add "in," simply use "enter."

22. Plan ahead.

You cannot plan for the past. Planning can only be done for the future. When you use "plan," the future is already implied.

23. Possibly might.

The words might and possibly signify probability, so just use one at a time.

24. Direct confrontation.

A confrontation is a head-on conflict, and does not need to be modified with "direct."

25. Postpone until later.

Something postponed is delayed or moved to a later time, and does not need to be modified with "later."

26. False pretense.

The word pretense is only used to describe a deception, so a "false" pretense is redundant.

27. Protest against.

Protest involves showing opposition; there is no need to use against.

28. End result.

Result only comes at the end. The reader who sees the word 'result' already knows that it occurs at the end.

29. Estimated at about/roughly.

Estimates are approximations that are not expected to be accurate, and do not need to be modified with "roughly" or "about."

30. Repeat again.

Repeat refers to something performed or occuring again and does not need to be modified with "again."

31. Difficult dilemma.

A dilemma is a situation that is complicated or difficult, and does not need to be modified with "difficult."

32. Revert back.

Revert indicates returning to a former or earlier state. Something that reverts goes back to how it used to be. No need to add back.

33. (During the) course (of).

During means "in or throughout the duration of," and doesn't require the use of the word "course."

34. Same identical.

Same and identical means the same thing and should not be used together.

35. Completely filled/finished/opposite.

Completely indicates thoroughness. However, the words finished and filled already indicate something thoroughly filled or finished to the extent possible. The words filled and finished thus do not need to be qualified with "completely."

36. Since the time when.

In this phrase, 'the time when' is not necessary as 'since' already indicates sometime in the past.

37. Close proximity/scrutiny.

Proximity means being close, in respect to location. Scrutiny means studying something closely. Both words suggest close, whether in respect to location as with proximity, or in respect to study, as with scrutiny. It is therefore unnecessary to use the words together.

38. Spell out in detail.

'Spell out' involves providing details, so no need to add "in detail."

39. Written down.

Anything written can be said to be taken down. Written should therefore be used on its own.

40. (Filled to) capacity.

Anything that is filled has reached its capacity and so the word capacity does not need to be used along with filled.

Speaking

THIS SECTION CONTAINS A SELF-ASSESSMENT AND SHORT SPEAKING TUTORIAL. The tutorial is designed to familiarize with general principles. So, while the self-assessment contains general questions similar to the questions likely to be on the CAEL®, but are not intended to be identical to the exam questions. If you do not understand parts of the tutorial, or find the tutorial difficult, it is recommended that you seek out additional instruction.

The CAEL® Speaking Questions

The Speaking section covers the following:

- Giving Advice
- Talking about Personal Experiences
- Describing a Scene in a Picture
- Making a Prediction about the Picture
- Comparing and Persuading
- Handling Difficulty Situations
- Expressing your Opinion

Speaking Review, Suggestions and Examples

Speaking - Example 1

Instructions:

Read the prompt below. You have 1 minute to prepare your response. You may make notes during this time.
After the preparation time, you will have 2 minutes to speak.

Talk about your pet, summer vacation, or similar

Example Response

I'm going to tell you about my weekend. Saturday I went to a friend's birthday party. She was turning forty and prepared an awesome party, full of people, music and food. I went with my boyfriend and we got there at 6 pm and left when the party ended, at about 10 pm. The place was full of people and there was so much food, they served grilled sandwiches, burgers and hot dogs, and they had several types of salad like Russian salad, Cesar salad, Cobb salad and Waldorf salad. The best part was the dessert: brownies, chocolate cake, vanilla cake, macaroons, s'mores dip and tons of cookies. It was the food heaven.

In addition they had a DJ mixing tunes live, so the music was fantastic. My boyfriend got so excited that he went to dance in the center of the dance floor, sadly he stumbled and fell in the middle of everyone. It was a little embarrassing, but a couple of burgers helped him recover from the "accident." When the party ended everyone went home happy and tired, we had a great time.

Sunday was calmer: my boyfriend and I went to the park with our dog, Sparks. Because Sparks is so big we couldn't take the bus, so we had to walk all the way to the park, but it was a sunny breeze day, so the walk was really nice. Sparks had so much fun playing with other dogs and with some kids. In the meantime my boyfriend and I sat in the grass to enjoy the sun. In our way back we stopped for ice-cream, Sparks ate a vanilla ice-cream, my boyfriend had a chocolate ice-cream and I ate a mint chocolate chips ice-cream. When we got home we just laid in bed watching movies until bed time. It was a good weekend.

Speaking - Example 2

Instructions:

Read the prompt below. You have 1 minute to prepare your response. You may make notes during this time.
After the preparation time, you will have 2 minutes to speak.

A friend is looking for a place to eat lunch, what to do on the weekend or similar.

Example Response

I have a really cool job: I'm a 3D artist. This means that I work with computer graphics to create digital spaces and characters in 3 dimensions, kind of what they do on Pixar. The difference between 2D and 3D animation is that in 3D you create an entire digital scene that can be seen from every angle and still make sense, which means that they obey the three known dimensions; height, width and depth. While 2D creates plain scenes that can only be watched from one angle in order to make sense. So, 3D animation has a perception similar to the one in the real world.

In 3D one starts with a blank space and has to create every single thing that goes in that space. For example, if you are creating a teenager's bedroom you must create everything that is in that room, including the room itself (I'm talking about the walls, door and windows), you will also have to make the furniture, like bed, desk and closet, and other things to fill the room like a computer, clothes, accessories, and anything you think the room needs. You also have to organize things within the room to make the scene look nice. This means that there are so many details to look after, and it takes time to make a single shot look really good. I specialize in hyper-realism, which means that I create scenes that look as close to the reality as possible. My line of work is really useful to create scenes that can't be done in the real world. The movie Avatar is a good example of hyper realistic 3D, but it's not necessary to have millions of dollars to create a good 3D scene. To be a good 3D artist you need to be patient and thoughtful, every one of your projects must be well thought and have as many worked details as you are able to give them.

Speaking - Giving Advice - Example 1

Instructions:

Read the prompt below. You have 1 minute to prepare your response. You may make notes during this time.
After the preparation time, you will have 2 minutes to speak.

A friend is looking for a place to eat lunch, what to do on the weekend or similar

Example response

There is a science to making desserts, some are really complicated and even the easiest ones have their tricks. Cakes are one of the most common desserts, it's a typical birthday celebration meal and there are tons and tons of types of cake you can make. Every type of cake has its particularities, but some things are general, like butter, flour, eggs and sugar. These are the ingredients of the classic cake, and it's trouble-free to make, but there are some tricks that can assure a professional cake.

Something really important is to make sure the butter is at room temperature, neither cold nor hot. Don't underestimate this because with the right temperature, the butter will mix better with the other ingredients. Another thing is to cream the sugar and butter thoroughly, make sure it becomes a creamy mix and that both ingredients are well mixed. A great recommendation for the eggs is to break them in a separate bowl, because if one is rotten it can ruin the whole mix. Also, add them one by one, so you can assure that every egg is well mixed before putting in the next.

For the flour there are two main rules: "mix" and "don't cream." The thing about flour is that if you cream it into the mix this will get too watery, and then you will have to put more flour in, to get the right consistency. This is a problem because when you bake, the cake will be too heavy.

And last, watch for the temperature in the oven, assure that the rack is right height, and don't open the oven every 5 minutes to check.

To tell if the cake its cooked, poke it in the center with a thin stick, if it comes out clean then the cake is ready, if the stick has raw mix on it, then you need to wait a few more minutes. Once the cake is ready wait, until it´s cool to take it out of the pan.

Speaking Giving Advice - Example 2

Instructions:

Read the prompt below. You have 1 minute to prepare your response. You may make notes during this time.
After the preparation time, you will have 2 minutes to speak.

Choosing an Apartment

Example Response

Choosing an apartment is a very personal decision that depends on your lifestyle and personal taste. So, to choose the right one for you, consider some a few of these points. First, you need to consider how close you want people to be, do you want neighbors to share with, or prefer a quiet place where you can work at peace? Also consider your family's needs, like if you have kids, you need to look for a safe neighborhood with schools nearby. These two considerations will define the best part of the city, and if you'll need a house or an apartment. Also, make a budget range, so you can look for places you can actually afford.

If you like to host friends or family you should select a place with wide common spaces, like a big kitchen or large living room, maybe an apartment with a porch where you can BBQ. On the other hand, if you are not interested in entertaining, then choose a place with a big bedroom and a great office, those can be more useful to you. If you enjoy the city life and to go out at night to a pub or to the movies make sure your place is in an area with lots of places and activities.

Another consideration is the way you'll get to work every day: if you have a car look for something with a parking lot preferably indoor, if you take the bus make sure you have a bus stop nearby. Also, try to not be too far from work or school, that way you'll reduce the time you spend moving from home to work or school and vice versa. Pets are something else to consider, because with a big dog you'll probably need a house with a patio, a smaller dog might not be a problem in an apartment but you'll still need to be close to a dog park or another space where you can take it for a walk.

Speaking - Example 1

Instructions:

Read the prompt below. You have 1 minute to prepare your response. You may make notes during this time.
After the preparation time, you will have 2 minutes to speak.

Talk about a great time you had with a family member or friend. Maybe you can talk about a party, something you did together at school, a time you travelled with a friend, or anything else you can remember. What happened and why was it memorable?

Example response

When I was a child my family and I lived 45-minutes from the beach, in a hot city with small buildings and streets paved with stones. Therefore, I learned about the sea and the sand when I was very small, and we visited the beach once every two weeks. The endless horizon of the sea was a wonder that I witnessed when I was young, and swimming in the waves was a familiar sensation. But I was eager to experience the opposite of my homeland - I wanted to go to the mountains and feel the snow.

When I was 14 my biggest dream came true: we went to the snowy mountains for a family vacation. It was one of the most amazing experiences of my life - looking at the world from a mountain top gives you a whole new perspective. For our trip we took the family car across 4 states, from the coast to the mountain chain. The first sight of the mountain landscape is something that I will never forget, to watch those gigantic mass climbing up to the clouds for the first time is breathtaking. As we got closer to the mountains I felt a change in the air, the cold air was refreshing and clean.

We finally got to mountains and got on the cable car that took us from the base of the mountain to the top, near the snowy peak. I had never felt so cold in my life, even though I had three sweaters, a mountain hat, snow gloves and warm boots on. I was quite scared on the climb, because we hung in a car over several precipices, but we got to the last station without any problem. We went out of the station and into the little balcony in groups, and finally were able to touch the snow.

It was incredible and frustrating at the same time. There was the snow, that I longed to meet for so long, but I was so cold that I couldn't even get one glove off to touch it with my own hands. It was like I couldn't live the entire experience because the direct contact wasn't possible.

That was at the time, later in my life I went again many times and I touched the snow, without caring for the cold. But the first encounter will always be in my heart an amazing and life-changing experience.

Speaking - Example 2

Instructions:

Read the prompt below. You have 1 minute to prepare your response. You may make notes during this time.
After the preparation time, you will have 2 minutes to speak.

Talk about a Personal Experience

Example Response

I think that welcoming new people into your life is a great possibility of change, independently of how that person came to you, if it was a college friend, a coworker, or a newborn in your family.

When my little sister was born I was 12 years-old, and I had been asking for a sibling since I was 6 or 7, to me the idea of having someone to care for and play with was like a dream come true. When it finally happened I was thinking less about playing and more about having someone to teach and share.

She was like a pink and warm ball that cried loudly once in a while, I felt in love at first sight. My mom didn't let me carry her for too long because she thought that my sister will not want to sleep in her cradle, but I was so excited about being with a big sis that I sneaked into her room and held her while she was sleep. My mom never noticed that I spoiled my sister like that, and after that she never had troubles sleeping in her cradle.

When my sister was born she changed my life entirely. I fell so much love for her, and now one of my top priorities is to keep her safe and happy. Its amazing how one person can change your entire universe to the point that you alter your life routine to spend time with that person, share experiences with her or him, and let that person be involved in your life. When a person is that important to you it can change the course of your life.

I think that it's great to welcome awesome people into your life that will help you grow and become a better version of yourself.

Speaking - Comparing and Persuading - Example 1

Instructions:

Read the prompt below. You have 1 minute to prepare your response. You may make notes during this time.
After the preparation time, you will have 2 minutes to speak.

Compare a motorcycle and a car

Example Response

A motorcycle and a car are types of motor vehicles that have similar engines, accelerator and brakes. The main difference is that the first has 2 wheels and the second has 4 wheels.

This might seem as a reduction of all the differences between them, but is in fact the main difference that opens the way to the others. Because of the different number of wheels, the physics that both vehicles obey are also totally different. For example, cars sustains its weight on its 4 wheels, the motorcycles sustain its weight in balance when rolling and on a leg when it stops. These differences also apply when they stop and turn; motorcycles can only require a small space to turn, while cars need a bigger space, and since motorcycles are lighter than the cars, they slow down faster. Also, a car is larger so it can carry many people, depending on the model, but generally at least 2 or 3. A motorcycle is smaller and can carry up to 2 people. This also means that a car is more expensive to maintain, as it needs more accessories and has more parts to maintain. Because it is larger, a car uses more fuel and resources than a motorcycle, and being an enclosed vehicle, it isolates the driver and the passengers from the environment.

On a motorcycle the driver and the passenger are on an open
vehicle, in direct contact with the road, which means they
are also at the mercy of the weather. As far as safety is concerned, it's not possible to say which vehicle is safer, since
they both have their own risks. Actually the safety of the
driver and passengers depends more on a responsible driver
than on the type of vehicle. Cars offer seat belts and air bags,
and motorcycle drivers need a helmet and other safety accessories. Both vehicles have advantages and disadvantages,
and to choosing between them depends on the particular
needs of the driver.

Speaking - Comparing and Persuading - Example 2

Instructions:

Read the prompt below. You have 1 minute to prepare your
response. You may make notes during this time.
After the preparation time, you will have 2 minutes to speak.

A romance movie and an action movie

Example Response

The only thing that romance films and action films have in
common is that both are movie genders, apart from that
they are almost completely different. A romance movie has
love and passion as the core of the story. The plot could be
about the lost of the loved one, or the moment they met, or
the difficulties of their relationship. As in every film, a romantic movie has an antagonist and obstacles, but the love
story defined these, which means that the antagonist won't
be someone who wants to take control of the world or something like that. Instead, it can be the father that won't let the
lovers be together, an illness that treated with separating the
lovers or a misunderstanding. Romantic movies are used to
explore the depths of love and the complications that can be
overcome with the faith in love. These movies are associated

with the examination of true feelings and concentrate on the inner world of the characters.
On the other hand, an action film is a movie where the challenges to the protagonist are the core of the story. These movies are often violent and have a lot of fights, as well as physical challenges that risk the characters' lives. The protagonist of these films is typically a hero or a regular person with the features of a hero that puts himself at risk to save another.

Another characteristic of these kind of movies is that the protagonist is usually a man, and rarely a woman. The villain can be someone who wants to take over the world, or that in somehow is a threat to a lot of people, which is why the hero must put himself at risk to save everyone. Since these are movies where the character is constantly at risk, its common to use computer-made effects to simulate some fights or risky sequences. These movies aren't specific about the inner world of the character, instead they center on the external action and don't go to deep about feelings, although they explore human reaction in extreme situations.

Speaking – Persuade your Friend to Choose – Example 1

Instructions:

Read the prompt below. You have 1 minute to prepare your response. You may make notes during this time.
After the preparation time, you will have 2 minutes to speak.

A motorcycle over a car

Example Response

A motorcycle is the right choice for you, it's way better then a car, believe me. First, take into account that you live in a city with a terrible traffic, people with cars spend a great deal of time stuck in traffic, which is terrible because you could use those 2 or 3 hours daily to do something more useful.

With a motorcycle you can avoid some traffic, it's not like you won't get stuck ever, it will be easier for you to stay away from main roads and you could go thought and around cars in a traffic jam. On the other hand, cars are expensive, and I'm not only talking about buying one, the maintenance is also very expensive: fuel, tires, and auto parts are expenses that you won't be able to avoid.

If you buy a new car the insurance can be really high, if you buy an older model then it will probably have a lot of parts that will need replacement soon. A motorcycle is much cheaper, it uses less fuel, has fewer parts, and needs fewer accessories. As with a car, if you buy a new motorcycle the insurance will be expensive, but still it will only be a fraction of a car's insurance. If you don't have the greatest salary a motorcycle is a better choice. In addition, why buy a car if you and your girlfriend will be the only ones in it? If you don't have a pet or relatives in town, so you don't need a vehicle with that much space. It would be a lot of space that you pay for, and that you maintain, but don't use. A motorcycle is way more practical for you, a case in the back where to keep your backpack or your groceries would be more than enough for you. Also, with the right motorcycle you can travel to the mountains and go through narrow dirt roads to explore, or go to the beach and go right to the water. A motorcycle is a much more versatile vehicle, and I think is the right one for you.

Persuade your Friend to Choose Example 2

Instructions:

Read the prompt below. You have 1 minute to prepare your response. You may make notes during this time.
After the preparation time, you will have 2 minutes to speak.

A romance movie over an action movie

Example Response

Since we're staying at home we should watch a romantic movie tonight and not an action movie - I think it will be the best choice. If you think about it, action films are always the same, there's no surprises there: the hero is going to save the world at the very last second, and he's going to get the girl.

There is nothing to think about when you are watching an action film, you could just listen to it and you would understand almost every scene. It's true that action films are fun and entertaining, but it would be better to watch it in a movie Theatre where we could enjoy the digital effects and feel surrounded with the sound. But to watch an action film at home isn't that much fun, the screen is way smaller and the sound isn't as good.

On the other hand, a romantic film will fit so much better in our plans. Since romantic films don't need big effects and doesn't have huge fights our small TV and our sound system will be more than enough for us to enjoy the movie. We could put the lights out, sit on the couch and just enjoy the film.

Besides, these films are really sentimental and there's a risk of crying, and I prefer to cry at home than in the Theatre. We should let the action movies for the cinema and take the private romantic films at home. Given that we are staying at home today I'm sure that the best choice is a romantic film.

Dealing with a Difficult Situation - Example 1

Instructions:

Read the prompt below. You have 1 minute to prepare your response. You may make notes during this time.
After the preparation time, you will have 2 minutes to speak.

My parents are getting divorced

Example response

A couple of months ago my parents told me that they are getting a divorce, and on the same day, my dad left the house and moved to an apartment. I know that divorce is something very common and that it doesn't mean that I don't have a family, but still I fell that everything was going to change and I don't want it to.

But that won't make a difference because it's really not my decision, and that's what bothers me the most. Despite how mad I'm with my parents I'm trying to be mature and do what's best for everyone, myself included. Some days ago I read an article that explained the things you need to do to better deal with a divorce. The first thing that they mentioned was to direct your anger, not towards your parents but with a hobby or exercise. I thought this was a great idea and started practicing yoga, it's been really helpful. Another interesting thing that the article explained was that you shouldn't take sides, what happened between your parents doesn't have to do with you, so you shouldn't get involved. If your parents love you equally you should do the same.

So, even though I'm mad with my mom for making my dad leave the house, I'm trying to understand her position and always keep in mind that she loves me. The article also talked about understanding, it explained that in this kind of situations everyone is very emotional, so we should try to be patience if your mom or dad is in a bad mood.

My mom has always been very understanding when it comes to my bad moods, so I'm being as supportive as I can, especially because I've seen her a little down lately. In addition to what I read in the article, I'm also talking about my feeling with my parents, I'm trying not to cling to negative feelings, instead, I'm communicating and this gave my parents the confidence to also communicate with me.

The first week I was really down, but this past week I've been feeling better, and now I really think everything is going to work out just fine.

Dealing with a difficult situation - Example 2

Instructions:

Read the prompt below. You have 1 minute to prepare your response. You may make notes during this time.
After the preparation time, you will have 2 minutes to speak.

I've failed my finals

Example Response

When you fail a test its bumps you down, but in my case I failed two final exams, which put me in a very bad position.

Aside the problems this failure brought me at school, my family is really disappointed and I don't feel good about myself at all. Right now I feel better, but the day I got the grades I felt like I was going to be a big failure and that I wasn't going to be successful at all. Despite how mad they were with me, my family was really supportive about it and tried to make me feel better.

But still I was upset and didn't know how to deal with it. As the days went by I realized that I can't let this failure be that important and become a reflection of my life; everybody fails, but what makes a winner is that they don't let the failure stop them. This wasn't the only chance life was going to give me, so I needed to stand up and prepare for the next time. I decided to change my attitude and try to make the most of a bad situation.

For starters, I need to learn from my mistakes, this way I won't stumble twice on the same rock. It also helps me think about where I want to be in 5 years, and, analyzed if those tests that I failed will stop me from achieving those goals.

This is a great way to project what I want and what I need to achieve to get it. And even though I shouldn't be rewarded for my bad grades, I like to get out and go for an ice-cream, to talk with a friend or just for a walk in the park. I've been really harsh on myself, and it's necessary to get distracted from those negative feeling for a while. And to not hold a grudge, I keep reminding myself that the tests are part of the learning process.

Practice Test Questions Set 1

The questions below are not the same as you will find on the CAEL® - that would be too easy! And nobody knows what the questions will be and they change all the time. Below are general questions that cover the same subject areas as the CAEL®. So, while the format and exact wording of the questions may differ slightly, and change from year to year, if you can answer the questions below, you will have no problem with the CAEL®.

For the best results, take these practice test questions as if it were the real exam. Set aside time when you will not be disturbed, and a location that is quiet and free of distractions. Read the instructions carefully, read each question carefully, and answer to the best of your ability.

Use the bubble answer sheets provided. When you have completed the Practice Questions, check your answer against the Answer Key and read the explanation provided.

Do not attempt more than one set of practice test questions in one day. After completing the first practice test, wait two or three days before attempting the second set of questions.

This practice test contains questions for the Listening and Reading sections. For practice with the Writing and Speaking, refer to the previous chapters.

Practice questions below are for the reading and listening sections. For practice with the speaking and writing sections see the examples above.

Note: If you have difficulty reading the QR codes, cover all the codes except the one you want and scan again.

Listening Answer Sheet

1. A B C D
2. A B C D
3. A B C D
4. A B C D
5. A B C D
6. A B C D
7. A B C D
8. A B C D
9. A B C D
10. A B C D
11. A B C D
12. A B C D
13. A B C D
14. A B C D
15. A B C D
16. A B C D
17. A B C D
18. A B C D
19. A B C D
20. A B C D
21. A B C D
22. A B C D
23. A B C D
24. A B C D
25. A B C D
26. A B C D
27. A B C D
28. A B C D
29. A B C D
30. A B C D
31. A B C D
32. A B C D
33. A B C D
34. A B C D
35. A B C D

Reading Answer Sheet

	A	B	C	D	E		A	B	C	D	E
1	○	○	○	○	○	21	○	○	○	○	○
2	○	○	○	○	○	22	○	○	○	○	○
3	○	○	○	○	○	23	○	○	○	○	○
4	○	○	○	○	○	24	○	○	○	○	○
5	○	○	○	○	○	25	○	○	○	○	○
6	○	○	○	○	○	26	○	○	○	○	○
7	○	○	○	○	○	27	○	○	○	○	○
8	○	○	○	○	○	28	○	○	○	○	○
9	○	○	○	○	○	29	○	○	○	○	○
10	○	○	○	○	○	30	○	○	○	○	○
11	○	○	○	○	○						
12	○	○	○	○	○						
13	○	○	○	○	○						
14	○	○	○	○	○						
15	○	○	○	○	○						
16	○	○	○	○	○						
17	○	○	○	○	○						
18	○	○	○	○	○						
19	○	○	○	○	○						
20	○	○	○	○	○						

Part I - Listening

Directions: Scan the QR codes or enter the URL into your browser to hear the audio. Choose the best choice for your answer.

Solving a Problem

Passage 1 Where to go for Dinner

Section I

Passage and Questions

1.
   a. They have paper menus
   b. They are looking online
   c. They aren't looking at menus
   d. None of the above

2.
   a. To McDonalds
   b. A cafeteria
   c. Somewhere not too fancy
   d. None of the above

3.

    a. Their budget was mid-range
    b. Their budget was high
    c. Their budget was low
    d. None of the above

Section 2

Passage and Question

4.

    a. Too Fancy
    b. Not pricey enough
    c. He doesn't like Italian food
    d. None of the above

5.

    a. Japanese
    b. Italian
    c. French
    d. None of the above

6.

    a. It was expensive
    b. It wasn't to fancy
    c. It was romantic
    d. None of the above

Section 3

Passage and Questions

7.

    a. He suggested French
    b. He suggested a compromise with Japanese
    c. He suggested not going for dinner that night
    d. None of the above

8.

    a. They would have more money
    b. They would have more time
    c. It wasn't so fancy
    d. None of the above

9.

    a. Yes they made a reservation for tonight
    b. They tried to make a reservation but couldn't
    c. No they didn't make a reservation
    d. None of the above.

Section II - Everyday Conversations

Getting the House Painted

Passage and Questions

10.

    a. He can't decide on color
    b. He thinks it is too expensive
    c. He doesn't think it needs it
    d. None of the above

11.

    a. Because she would like another color
    b. Because she doesn't want to go to Mexico
    c. Because the neighbours did and it looks bad
    d. None of the above

12.

    a. Clean
    b. Dirty
    c. Wrong color
    d. None of the above

Painting the House - Section 2

Passage and Questions

13.

    a. Yes
    b. No
    c. We don't know

14.

    a. In the yellow pages
    b. They know someone
    c. Ask the neighbours
    d. None of the above

15.

    a. They aren't going to
    b. In 2 weeks
    c. In 1 week
    d. None of the above

Listening for Information

Passage 1 - Fire

Passage and Questions

16.

  a. Yes
  b. No

17.

    a. The heat of the fire
    b. The material burning
    c. Impurities in the surrounding air
    d. None of the above.

Passage 2 - Gardens

Passage and Questions

18.

    a. Statues and Sculptures

    b. Flower beds

    c. Medicinal Herbs

    d. Courtyard gardens

19.

    a. Before the Fall of Rome.

    b. Gardening did not decline.

    c. Before the Middle Ages.

    d. After the Fall of Rome.

20.

    a. Gardening with hedges and vines

    b. Gardening with a wide variety of flowers

    c. Gardening for medicinal plants and decorating churches

    d. Gardening divided by watercourse

Passage 3 - Insect Pests

Passage and Questions

21.

      a. By training them
      b. Using insecticides and other techniques
      c. In many different ways
      d. Humans don't control insects

22.

      a. Cows and bats
      b. Bees and silkworms
      c. Caterpillars and ants
      d. None of the above

23.

      a. 5%
      b. 10%
      c. 1%
      d. 3%

Listening to News

Passage 1 - Fire Extinguishers

Passage and Questions

24.

    a. Electrical fires

    b. Out of control fires

    c. Fires on a boat or marina

    d. None of the above

25.

    a. Every 6 months

    b. There is no set time

    c. Every year

    d. Every 5 years

26.

    a. Stored pressure and cartridge-operated

    b. Chemical and water based

    c. Chemical and gas such as CO_2

    d. None of the above

27.

    a. 20 pounds
    b. 1 - 30 pounds
    c. 10 pounds
    d. 50 pounds

Listening for a Point of View

Passage 1 - Bitcoin

Passage and Questions

28.

    a. That bitcoin will replace all currencies
    b. That bitcoin has a central bank
    c. That bitcoin does not use a lot of electricity
    d. None of the above

29.

    a. Bitcoin is dangerous
    b. Bitcoin is used for illegal purchases
    c. Bitcoin only uses a small amount of electricity
    d. None of the above

30.

    a. Bitcoin will replace the banking and financial system
    b. Bitcoin will only replace parts of the banking system
    c. Bitcoin must have a central bank
    d. None of the above

Reading

Directions: The following questions are based on several reading passages. Each passage is followed by a series of questions. Read each passage carefully, and then answer the questions based on it. You may reread the passage as often as you wish. When you have finished answering the questions based on one passage, go right onto the next passage. Choose the best answer based on the information given.

Questions 1 – 3 refer to the following passage.

Passage 1 - 3 The Life of Helen Keller

Many people have heard of Helen Keller. She is famous because she was unable to see or hear, but learned to speak and read and went onto attend college and earn a degree. Her life is a very interesting story, one that she developed into an autobiography, which was then adapted into both a stage play and a movie. How did Helen Keller overcome her disabilities to become a famous woman? Read onto find out.
Helen Keller was not born blind and deaf. When she was a small baby, she had a very high fever for several days. As a result of her sudden illness, baby Helen lost her eyesight and her hearing. Because she was so young when she went deaf and blind, Helen Keller never had any recollection of being able to see or hear. Since she could not hear, she could not learn to talk. Since she could not see, it was difficult for her to move around. For the first six years of her life, her world was very still and dark.

Imagine what Helen's childhood must have been like. She could not hear her mother's voice. She could not see the beauty of her parent's farm. She could not recognize who was giving her a hug, or a bath or even where her bedroom was each night. More sad, she could not communicate with her parents in any way. She could not express her feelings or tell them the things she wanted. It must have been a very sad childhood.

When Helen was six years old, her parents hired her a teacher named Anne Sullivan. Anne was a young woman who was almost blind. However, she could hear and she could read Braille, so she was a perfect teacher for young Helen. At first, Anne had a very hard time teaching Helen anything. She described her first impression of Helen as a "wild thing, not a child." Helen did not like Anne at first either. She bit and hit Anne when Anne tried to teach her. However, the two of them eventually came to have a great deal of love and respect.

Anne taught Helen to hear by putting her hands on people's throats. She could feel the sounds that people made. In time, Helen learned to feel what people said. Next, Anne taught Helen to read Braille, which is a way that books are written for the blind. Finally, Anne taught Helen to talk. Although Helen did learn to talk, it was hard for anyone but Anne to understand her.

As Helen grew older, more and more people were amazed by her story. She went to college and wrote books about her life. She gave talks to the public, with Anne at her side, translating her words. Today, both Anne Sullivan and Helen Keller are famous women who are respected for their lives' work.

1. Helen Keller could not see and hear and so, what was her biggest problem in childhood?

    a. Inability to communicate

    b. Inability to walk

    c. Inability to play

    d. Inability to eat

2. Helen learned to hear by feeling the vibrations people made when they spoke. What were these vibrations were felt through?

    a. Mouth

    b. Throat

    c. Ears

    d. Lips

3. What has Helen Keller's story been adapted for?

   a. A movie and a play
   b. A movie
   c. A play
   d. Her story hasn't been adapted

Questions 4 – 5 refer to the following passage.

Passage 2 - Ways Characters Communicate in Theatre

Playwrights give their characters voices in a way that gives depth and added meaning to what happens on stage during their play. There are different types of speech in scripts that allow characters to talk with themselves, with other characters, and even with the audience.

It is very unique to Theatre that characters may talk "to themselves." When characters do this, the speech they give is called a soliloquy. Soliloquies are usually poetic, introspective, moving, and can tell audience members about the feelings, motivations, or suspicions of an individual character without that character having to reveal them to other characters on stage. "To be or not to be" is a famous soliloquy given by Hamlet as he considers difficult but important themes, such as life and death.

The most common type of communication in plays is when one character is speaking to another or a group of other characters. This is generally called dialogue, but can also be called monologue if one character speaks without being interrupted for a long time. It is not necessarily the most important type of communication, but it is the most common because the plot of the play cannot really progress without it.
Lastly, and most unique to Theatre (although it has been used somewhat in film) is when a character speaks directly to the audience. This is called an aside, and scripts usually specifically direct actors to do this. Asides are usually com-

ical, an inside joke between the character and the audience, and very short. The actor will usually face the audience when delivering them, even if it's for a moment, so the audience can recognize this move as an aside.

All three of these types of communication are important to the art of Theatre, and have been perfected by famous playwrights like Shakespeare. Understanding these types of communication can help an audience member grasp what is artful about the script and action of a play.

4. According to the passage, characters in plays communicate to

    a. move the plot forward

    b. show the private thoughts and feelings of one character

    c. make the audience laugh

    d. add beauty and artistry to the play

5. What do Soliloquies tell us?

    a. When a character is speaking to a group

    b. About the feelings and motivations of a character

    c. How the plot is moving forward

    d. None of the above

Questions 6 – 8 refer to the following passage.

Passage 3 - Low Blood Sugar

As the name suggest, low blood sugar is low sugar levels in the bloodstream. This can occur when you have not eaten properly and undertake strenuous activity, or, when you are very hungry. When Low blood sugar occurs regularly and is ongoing, it is a medical condition called hypoglycemia. This condition can occur in diabetics and in healthy adults.

Causes of low blood sugar can include excessive alcohol consumption, metabolic problems, stomach surgery, pancreas, liver or kidneys problems, as well as a side-effect of some medications.

Symptoms

There are different symptoms depending on the severity of the case.

Mild hypoglycaemia can lead to feelings of nausea and hunger. The patient may also feel nervous, jittery and have fast heart beats. Sweaty skin, clammy and cold skin are likely symptoms.

Moderate hypoglycaemia can result in a short temper, confusion, nervousness, fear and blurring of vision. The patient may feel weak and unsteady.

Severe cases of hypoglycaemia can lead to seizures, coma, fainting spells, nightmares, headaches, excessive sweats and severe tiredness.

Diagnosis of low blood sugar

A doctor can diagnosis this medical condition by asking the patient questions and testing blood and urine samples. Home testing kits are available for patients to monitor blood sugar levels. It is important to see a qualified doctor though. The doctor can administer tests to ensure that will safely rule out other medical conditions that could affect blood sugar levels.

Treatment

Quick treatments include drinking or eating foods and drinks with high sugar contents. Good examples include soda, fruit juice, hard candy and raisins. Glucose energy tablets can also help. Doctors may also recommend medications and well as changes in diet and exercise routine to treat chronic low blood sugar.

6. Based on the article, which of the following is true?

    a. Low blood sugar can happen to anyone.

    b. Low blood sugar only happens to diabetics.

    c. Low blood sugar can occur even.

    d. None of the statements are true.

7. Which of the following are the author's opinion?

    a. Quick treatments include drinking or eating foods and drinks with high sugar contents.

    b. None of the statements are opinions.

    c. This condition can occur in diabetics and also in healthy adults.

    d. There are different symptoms depending on the severity of the case

8. Why is it important to see a doctor?

    a. To give tests
    b. To monitor blood sugar levels
    c. To rule out other medical conditions
    d. None of the above

Questions 9 – 11 refer to the following passage.

How To Get A Good Nights Sleep

Sleep is just as essential for healthy living as water, air and food. Sleep allows the body to rest and replenish depleted energy levels. Sometimes we may for various reasons experience difficulty sleeping which has a serious effect on our health. Those who have prolonged sleeping problems are facing a serious medical condition and should see a qualified doctor when possible for help. Here is simple guide that can help you sleep better at night.

Try to create a natural pattern of waking up and sleeping around the same time everyday. This means avoiding going to bed too early and oversleeping past your usual wake up time. Going to bed and getting up at radically different times everyday confuses your body clock. Try to establish a natural rhythm as much as you can.

Exercises and a bit of physical activity can help you sleep better at night. If you are having problem sleeping, try to be as active as you can during the day. If you are tired from physical activity, falling asleep is a natural and easy process for your body. If you remain inactive during the day, you will find it harder to sleep properly at night. Try walking, jogging, swimming or simple stretches as you get close to your bed time.

Afternoon naps are great to refresh you during the day, but they may also keep you awake at night. If you feel sleepy during the day, get up, take a walk and get busy to keep from sleeping. Stretching is a good way to increase blood flow to the brain and keep you alert so that you don't sleep during the day. This will help you sleep better night.

> A warm bath or a glass of milk in the evening can help your body relax and prepare for sleep. A cold bath will wake you up and keep you up for several hours. Also avoid eating too late before bed.

9. How would you describe this sentence?

    a. A recommendation

    b. An opinion

    c. A fact

    d. A diagnosis

10. What is a disadvantage of taking naps?

    a. They may keep you awake.

    b. There are no disadvantages

    c. They may help you sleep better

    d. They may affect your diet

11. What is one of the recommendations to get a better night's sleep?

    a. Exercise

    b. Afternoon naps

    c. Drinking Alcohol

    d. None of the above

Questions 12 – 25 refer to the following email.

SUBJECT: MEDICAL STAFF CHANGES

To all staff:

This email is to advise you of a paper on recommended medical staff changes has been posted to the Human Resources website.

The contents are of primary interest to medical staff, other staff may be interested in reading it, particularly those in medical support roles.

The paper deals with several major issues:

    1. Improving our ability to attract top quality staff to the hospital, and retain our existing staff. These changes will make our position and departmental names internationally recognizable and comparable with North American and North Asian departments and positions.

2. Improving our ability to attract top quality staff by introducing greater flexibility in the departmental structure.

3. General comments on issues to be further discussed in relation to research staff.

The changes outlined in this paper are significant. I encourage you to read the document and send to me any comments you may have, so that it can be enhanced and improved.

Gordon Simms
Administrator,
Seven Oaks Regional Hospital

12. Are all hospital staff required to read the document posted to the Human Resources website?

    a. Yes all staff are required to read the document.

    b. No, reading the document is optional.

    c. Only medical staff are required to read the document.

    d. none of the above are correct.

13. Have the changes to medical staff been made?

    a. Yes, the changes have been made.

    b. No, the changes are only being discussed.

    c. Some of the changes have been made.

    d. None of the choices are correct.

14. Is the email concerned about attracting new staff primarily, or retaining existing staff?

    a. Primarily attracting new staff

    b. Primarily to retain existing staff

    c. Both attract new staff and retain existing staff

    d. None of the above

Here is a response to the email above. Questions 15 - 20.

Mr. Simms:

Thank you for the email and the ____15____. Some of the people in my department, and I have some recommendations for ____16____, and would like to ____17____.

Talking with my co-workers, we feel there are a number of things ____18____ from your paper, and we would like to ____19____.

We look forward to ____20____, when it is convenient for you.

Yours,

Marsha Jones
Head Nurse

15.

    a. Recommended changes
    b. Changes
    c. Consultations
    d. None of the above

16.

    a. Existing staff
    b. New staff
    c. Both existing and new staff
    d. None of the above

17.

    a. Meet with you to discuss
    b. Discuss with each other
    c. Meet with someone
    d. None of the above

18.

    a. Included
    b. Missing
    c. Mentioned
    d. None of the above

19.

    a. Discuss
    b. Omit
    c. Visit
    d. None of the above

20.

    a. Meeting
    b. Reading the report
    c. Discussing the report
    d. None of the above

Questions 21 - 24 refer to the following passage.

Some people, and many environmentalists think that oil and gas, and fossil fuels in general are unsustainable and need to be replaced by renewable sources of energy. Fossil fuels pollute the atmosphere and cause climate change. Researchers and scientists all over the world have discovered cost effective and non-polluting sources of energy such as wind and solar power, as well as more exotic energy sources such as tidal power and geothermal.

Critics say alternative energy sources are much more expensive and can never replace oil and gas, fossil fuels. Certainly this has been the case for many years but recently that has changed dramatically. With the recent increases in oil and gas prices, and reduction in the cost renewable energy, it has reached the 'tipping point' where it is the same cost or cheaper than fossil fuels.

Another criticism of alternative energy is that it will cost jobs. This is a common misunderstanding. In fact, the renewable energy sector employs more people than the oil and gas sector.

For all these reasons, renewable energy has a bright future!

21. The author of this article believes,

    a. Renewable sources are better than fossil fuel

    b. Fossil fuels are better than renewable sources

    c. Both renewables and fossil fuels are good sources of energy

    d. The author is not endorsing either choice

22. How does the author respond to critics that say renewable energy is more expensive?

a. By pointing out that recently renewables have become cost effective

b. The author does not respond to this criticism

c. By pointing out that recently fossil fuel has become cost effective

d. None of the above

23. When has/will renewables become more cost-effective than fossil fuel?

a. Renewables became more cost effective years ago

b. Renewable have only recently become more cost effective

c. Renewable will never be more cost effective

d. None of the above

24. What has happened to the price of fossil fuel to make renewables more cost-effective?

a. The cost of fossil fuels have decreased

b. The cost of fossil fuels have increased

c. The cost of fossil fuels has stayed about the same

d. None of the above

Response to this article - Questions 25 - 30

I read your article with interest. I disagree on many points though. Yes, renewables are getting cheaper and are very useful, but we ___25___. Tens of thousands of people work in the oil and gas sector and ___26___ do you suggest they will go?

Do you ___27___ think alternative energy can take over everything? I don't think so! What about northern cities with very little ____28____? There are many examples where renewables simply would not work.

Plus, I think fossil fuels, with all their problems, are everywhere. Replacing ____29____ as a source of energy is a ____30____ and is not going to happen overnight if at all.

25.

    a. Must switch to renewables
    b. Can afford to pay for fossil fuel
    c. Still need oil and gas
    d. None of the above

26.

    a. Who
    b. What
    c. Where
    d. None of the above

27.

    a. Not
    b. Really
    c. None of the above

28.

    a. Oil
    b. Sunshine
    c. Telephone service
    d. None of the above

29.

    a. Fossil fuel
    b. Renewables
    c. Sunshine
    d. None of the above

30.

    a. Huge job
    b. Small job
    c. Not possible
    d. None of the above

Answer Key

Listening

1. B
They are looking at menus online

2. C
The man wants to go somewhere not too fancy

3. A
Their budget was mid-range.

4. A
He didn't want Italian or French because it was too fancy.

5. C
She wanted a French restaurant.

6. C
She liked the French restaurant because it was romantic.

7. B
He suggested a compromise with going to a Japanese restaurant that night and the French one on the weekend.

8. B
Saturday was better for the French restaurant because they would have more time.

9. C
No they didn't make a reservation for tonight. They are going to make a reservation for Saturday.

10. B
He isn't sure about painting the house because he feels it is to expensive.

11. C
She wants the house painted because it looks grubby and the neighbours had their house painted.

12. B
Grubby means dirty.

13. A
Yes, the house bothers the man as well

14. B
They are going to find a painter by asking the neighbours

15. C
They are going to talk about it in 1 week.

16. B
Fire is an oxidation process but is much faster than rust or digestion.

17. B
Depending on the materials burning, the flame is a different color.

18. A
Roman gardens are known for their statues and sculptures.

19. D
After the fall of Rome, gardening declined.

20. C
From the passage, "during the Middle Ages, gardening was strictly for herbs used in various medicines, and for decorating churches."

21. B
The techniques for controlling insects is taken from the last paragraph.

22. B
Bees and silkworms are examples of beneficial insects.

23. C
1% of the insect family are pests.

24. B
Fire extinguishers are typically used for small fires and not intended for out-of-control fires, such as one which has reached the ceiling, or endangers the user.

25. C
Fire extinguishers are typically inspected every year, although some jurisdictions require more frequent inspections.

26. A
The two most common types of fire extinguishers are stored pressure and cartridge-operated.

27. A
Hand-held fire extinguishers weigh between 1 and 30 pounds.

28. A
Proponents believe bitcoin will replace all currencies

29. B
Critics believe bitcoin is used for illegal purchases. Choice A is a possibility, but isn't stated in the passage - choice B is still the best choice.

30. A
Bitcoin enthusiasts say bitcoin will eventually replace the banking and financial system. Choice B is a partly true but not mentioned in the passage - Choice A is the best choice.

Part II – Reading Comprehension

1. A
Helen's parents hired Anne to teach Helen to communicate. Choice B is incorrect because the passage states Anne had trouble finding her way around, which means she could walk. Choice C is incorrect because you don't hire a teacher to teach someone to play. Choice D is incorrect because by age 6, if Helen had never eaten, she would have starved to death.

2. B
The correct answer because that fact is stated directly in the passage. The passage explains that Anne taught Helen to hear by allowing her to feel the vibrations in her throat.

3. A
Her story has been adapted to a movie and a play.

4. D
The question is asking very generally about the message of the passage, and the title, "Ways Characters Communicate

in Theatre," is one indication of that. The other choices A, B, and C are all directly from the text, and therefore readers may be inclined to select one of them, but are too specific to encapsulate the entirety of the passage and its message.

5. B
From the passage, "Soliloquies are usually poetic, introspective, moving, and can tell audience members about the feelings, motivations, or suspicions of an individual character …"

6. A
Low blood sugar occurs both in diabetics and healthy adults.

7. B
None of the statements are the author's opinion.

8. C
It is important to see a doctor to rule out other medical conditions.

9. A
This sentence is a recommendation.

10. A
From the passage, one disadvantage of taking naps is they may keep you awake at night.

11. A
One of the recommendations for a better night's sleep is exercises and a bit of physical activity.

12. B
Reading the document posted to the Human Resources website is optional.

13. B
The document is recommended changes and have not be implemented yet.

14. C
The changes are to both attract new staff and retain existing staff.

15. A
Recommended changes is the best answer. Choice B, changes, is close but choice A is better. Choice C, consultations is not relevant.

16. A
Choice A, existing staff is the best choice since she refers to other people in her department. The other choices are not relevant.

17. A
Here she is wanting to meet with Mr. Simms. Clearly choice B is not relevant, since they have already discussed with each other. Choice C is also not relevant, since they are emailing Mr. Simms.

18. B
Here she is referring to things that are missing from the paper. The other choices can be eliminated, when considering the context.

19. A
Discuss, choice A is the best choice. Clearly choice B is incorrect as she doesn't want to omit, and also choice C, visit, doesn't make sense in this sentence.

20. A
Here she is looking forward to meeting, as previously mentioned in her reply. Choice B is incorrect, since she has already read the report. Choice C is incorrect since she wants to discuss changes and additions to the report.

21. A
The author is clearly in favour of renewable energy over fossil fuels.

22. A
The author responds to this criticism by pointing out that recently renewables have become cost effective.

23. B
Renewables have become more cost effective recently, as their cost as gone done and the cost of fossil fuel has gone up.

24. B
The cost of fossil fuel has increased.

25. C
Since this person is generally opposed to renewables, the only answer in this context is choice C, still need oil and gas.

26. C
In the context of the sentence, 'where' is the only correct choice.

27. B
'Really' in this sentence is the only answer that makes sense.

28. B
Here the sentence is a questions asking about northern towns and since the response is against renewables, the only answer is choice B, sunshine.

29. A
Here the sentence is a questions about replacing something, and since the article is against renewables, in this context the sentence is about replacing fossil fuels with renewables.

30. A
Here the sentence talks about replacing fossil fuel and further says it won't happen overnight. Choice A 'huge job' is the best choice.

Analyzing your practice tests

Go through your answers carefully. For each wrong answer, refer to the explanations, and work through the questions step-by-step.

What kind of question are you getting wrong? (e.g. reading comprehension, science, algebra, basic math etc.)

Look for patterns in your incorrect answers. What is it *exactly* that you are doing wrong or don't understand.

What types of questions do you have the most difficulty with? Refer to the tutorials and try to understand the reasoning that gives the correct answer.

Refer back to chapter one and re-do your study schedule

Practice Test Questions Set 2

The questions below are not the same as you will find on the CAEL® - that would be too easy! And nobody knows what the questions will be and they change all the time. Below are general questions that cover the same subject areas as the CAEL®. So, while the format and exact wording of the questions may differ slightly, and change from year to year, if you can answer the questions below, you will have no problem with the CAEL®.

For the best results, take these practice test questions as if it were the real exam. Set aside time when you will not be disturbed, and a location that is quiet and free of distractions. Read the instructions carefully, read each question carefully, and answer to the best of your ability.

Use the bubble answer sheets provided. When you have completed the Practice Questions, check your answer against the Answer Key and read the explanation provided.

Do not attempt more than one set of practice test questions in one day.

After completing the first practice test, wait two or three days before attempting the second set of questions.

Practice questions below are for the reading and listening sections. For practice with the speaking and writing sections see the examples above.

NOTE: **If you have difficulty scanning, cover all the codes except the one you want and try again.**

Listening

	A	B	C	D	E		A	B	C	D	E
1	○	○	○	○	○	21	○	○	○	○	○
2	○	○	○	○	○	22	○	○	○	○	○
3	○	○	○	○	○	23	○	○	○	○	○
4	○	○	○	○	○	24	○	○	○	○	○
5	○	○	○	○	○	25	○	○	○	○	○
6	○	○	○	○	○	26	○	○	○	○	○
7	○	○	○	○	○	27	○	○	○	○	○
8	○	○	○	○	○	28	○	○	○	○	○
9	○	○	○	○	○	29	○	○	○	○	○
10	○	○	○	○	○	30	○	○	○	○	○
11	○	○	○	○	○						
12	○	○	○	○	○						
13	○	○	○	○	○						
14	○	○	○	○	○						
15	○	○	○	○	○						
16	○	○	○	○	○						
17	○	○	○	○	○						
18	○	○	○	○	○						
19	○	○	○	○	○						
20	○	○	○	○	○						

Reading

1. Ⓐ Ⓑ Ⓒ Ⓓ   18. Ⓐ Ⓑ Ⓒ Ⓓ
2. Ⓐ Ⓑ Ⓒ Ⓓ   19. Ⓐ Ⓑ Ⓒ Ⓓ
3. Ⓐ Ⓑ Ⓒ Ⓓ   20. Ⓐ Ⓑ Ⓒ Ⓓ
4. Ⓐ Ⓑ Ⓒ Ⓓ   21. Ⓐ Ⓑ Ⓒ Ⓓ
5. Ⓐ Ⓑ Ⓒ Ⓓ   22. Ⓐ Ⓑ Ⓒ Ⓓ
6. Ⓐ Ⓑ Ⓒ Ⓓ   23. Ⓐ Ⓑ Ⓒ Ⓓ
7. Ⓐ Ⓑ Ⓒ Ⓓ   24. Ⓐ Ⓑ Ⓒ Ⓓ
8. Ⓐ Ⓑ Ⓒ Ⓓ   25. Ⓐ Ⓑ Ⓒ Ⓓ
9. Ⓐ Ⓑ Ⓒ Ⓓ   26. Ⓐ Ⓑ Ⓒ Ⓓ
10. Ⓐ Ⓑ Ⓒ Ⓓ   27. Ⓐ Ⓑ Ⓒ Ⓓ
11. Ⓐ Ⓑ Ⓒ Ⓓ   28. Ⓐ Ⓑ Ⓒ Ⓓ
12. Ⓐ Ⓑ Ⓒ Ⓓ   29. Ⓐ Ⓑ Ⓒ Ⓓ
13. Ⓐ Ⓑ Ⓒ Ⓓ   30. Ⓐ Ⓑ Ⓒ Ⓓ
14. Ⓐ Ⓑ Ⓒ Ⓓ   31. Ⓐ Ⓑ Ⓒ Ⓓ
15. Ⓐ Ⓑ Ⓒ Ⓓ   32. Ⓐ Ⓑ Ⓒ Ⓓ
16. Ⓐ Ⓑ Ⓒ Ⓓ   33. Ⓐ Ⓑ Ⓒ Ⓓ
17. Ⓐ Ⓑ Ⓒ Ⓓ   34. Ⓐ Ⓑ Ⓒ Ⓓ
              35. Ⓐ Ⓑ Ⓒ Ⓓ

Part I - Listening

Directions: Scan the QR codes or enter the URL into your browser to hear the audio. Choose the best choice for your answer. **NOTE:** If you have difficulty scanning, cover all the codes except you want and try again.

Solving a Problem - Connecting to the Internet

Calling technician on the phone to connect to the Internet.

Section I

Passage and Questions

1.
   a. She is trying to connect to the internet first
   b. She is trying to connect her phone first
   c. She is trying to connect her husbands computer
   d. None of the above

2.
   a. She doesn't know
   b. She has a wired connection
   c. She has both
   d. None of the above

3.

    a. She can't tell
    b. She couldn't find it
    c. She has a large blue wire at the back of her computer
    d. None of the above

Solving a Problem - Section II

Passage and Questions

4.

    a. It was a different version
    b. The instructions were incorrect
    c. There wasn't one
    d. None of the above

5.

    a. He didn't have a suggestion
    b. Clicking on the Start button
    c. Clicking on the Settings button
    d. None of the above

6.

    a. Yes there were several
    b. She couldn't find it
    c. No there weren't any networks
    d. None of the above

Solving a Problem - Section III

Passage and Questions

7.

    a. Yes
    b. No

8.

    a. They didn't have to check
    b. They couldn't check
    c. They opened a browser
    d. None of the above

9.

    a. Yahoo
    b. Google
    c. CNN
    d. None of the above

Part II - Everyday Conversation

Driving to Work

Passage and Questions

10.

    a. He couldn't drive

    b. He wanted a break

    c. She always drove

    d. None of the above

11.

    a. Lots of meetings

    b. A busy day

    c. The project at his work wasn't going well

    d. None of the above

12.

    a. The project at her work was not going well

    b. She had meetings all day

    c. Nothing was bothering her

    d. None of the above

13.

    a. Saturday and Sunday

    b. Saturday and maybe Sunday

    c. He wasn't going to have to work this weekend

    d. None of the above

14.

    a. Go to a movie

    b. Nothing special

    c. Do something fun

    d. None of the above

Part III - Listening to News

Passage and Questions

15.

    a. He was at home

    b. He was going to school

    c. He was going home

    d. He was going downtown

16.

    a. He went into rescue the baby and grandmother

    b. He called the emergency services

    c. He went home to call the emergency services

    d. None of the above

17.

    a. The fire department was busy

    b. It did not take a long time

    c. I take a long time because the house was out of town

    d. None of the above

Listening for Information

Passage 1 - Volcanoes

Passage and Questions

18.

    a. Underwater

    b. On land

    c. In Europe

    d. In the US

19. What causes volcanoes?

    a. Magma

    b. A split in the earth's plates

    c. Escaping gas

    c. None of the above

Passage 2 - Types of Volcanoes

Passage and Questions

20.

    a. It covered the city of Pompeii

    b. It cooled the global temperature

    c. It was not a big explosion

    d. None of the above

21.

    a. In the Arctic

    b. In Russia

    c. In the Hawaiian Islands

    d. In Canada

22.

    a. Supervolcanoes

    b. Conical mountains of lava

    c. Underwater volcanoes

    d. Lava domes

23.

    a. Yes

    b. No

Passage 3 Wild Animals in Urban Areas

Passage and Questions

24.

    a. Deer

    b. Mountain Lions

    c. Wolves

    d. Rabbits

25.

    a. Yes

    b. No

Listening to a Point of View

Passage 1 - Studying

26.

    a. He doesn't say
    b. People who are distracted easily
    c. People who listen to music
    d. None of the above

27.

    a. Yes
    b. No

28.

    a. Hands on
    b. Distracted
    c. Poor learner
    d. None of the above

29.

    a. Playing music
    b. Making it into a game
    c. The author does not have recommendations
    d. None of the above

30.

    a. The author likes background music while studying
    b. The author does not like background music while studying
    c. The author does not have an opinion
    d. None of the above

Reading Comprehension

Directions: The following questions are based on several reading passages. Each passage is followed by a series of questions. Read each passage carefully, and then answer the questions based on it. You may reread the passage as often as you wish. When you have finished answering the questions based on one passage, go right onto the next passage. Choose the best answer based on the information given.

Questions 1 - 3 refer to the following passage.

Chocolate Chip Cookies

3/4 cup sugar
       3/4 cup packed brown sugar
       1 cup butter, softened
       2 large eggs, beaten
       1 teaspoon vanilla extract
       2 1/4 cups all-purpose flour
       1 teaspoon baking soda
       3/4 teaspoon salt
       2 cups semisweet chocolate chips

If desired, 1 cup chopped pecans, or chopped walnuts

Preheat oven to 375 degrees. Mix sugar, brown sugar, butter, vanilla and eggs in a large bowl. Stir in flour, baking soda, and salt. The dough will be very stiff.

Stir in chocolate chips by hand with a sturdy wooden spoon. Add the pecans, or other nuts, if desired. Stir until the chocolate chips and nuts are evenly dispersed.

Drop dough by rounded tablespoonfuls 2 inches apart onto a cookie sheet.

Bake 8 to 10 minutes or, until light brown. Cookies may look underdone, but they will finish cooking after you take them out of the oven.

1. What is the correct order for adding these ingredients?

   a. Brown sugar, baking soda, chocolate chips
   b. Baking soda, brown sugar, chocolate chips
   c. Chocolate chips, baking soda, brown sugar
   d. Baking soda, chocolate chips, brown sugar

2. What does dispersed mean?

   a. Scatter
   b. To form a ball
   c. To stir
   d. To beat

3. When can you stop stirring the nuts?

   a. When the cookies are cooked.
   b. When the nuts are evenly distributed.
   c. As soon as the nuts are added.
   d. After the chocolate chips are added.

Questions 4 - 6 refer to the following passage.

Passage 1 - The Crusades

In 1095 Pope Urban II proclaimed the First Crusade with the intent and stated goal to restore Christian access to holy places in and around Jerusalem. Over the next 200 years there were 6 major crusades and numerous minor crusades in the fight for control of the "Holy Land." Historians are divided on the real purpose of the Crusades, some believing that it was part of a purely defensive war against Islamic conquest; some see them as part of a long-running conflict at the frontiers of Europe; and others see them as confident, aggressive, papal-led expansion attempts by Western Christendom. The impact of the crusades was profound, and judgment of the Crusaders ranges from laudatory to highly critical. However, all agree that the Crusades and wars waged during those crusades were brutal and often bloody. Several hundred thousand Roman Catholic Christians joined the Crusades, they were Christians from all over Europe.

Europe at the time was under the Feudal System, so while the Crusaders made vows to the Church they also were beholden to their Feudal Lords. This led to the Crusaders not only fighting the Saracen, the commonly used word for Muslim at the time, but also each other for power and economic gain in the Holy Land. This infighting between the Crusaders is why many historians hold the view that the Crusades were simply a front for Europe to invade the Holy Land for economic gain in the name of the Church. Another factor contributing to this theory is that while the army of crusaders marched towards Jerusalem they pillaged the land as they went. The church and feudal Lords vowing to return the land to its original beauty, and inhabitants, this rarely happened though as the Lords often kept the land for themselves. A full 800 years after the Crusades, Pope John Paul II expressed his sorrow for the massacre of innocent people and the lasting damage the Medieval church caused in that area of the World.

4. What is the tone of this article?

    a. Subjective

    b. Objective

    c. Persuasive

    d. None of the Above

5. What can all historians agree on concerning the Crusades?

    a. It achieved great things

    b. It stabilized the Holy Land

    c. It was bloody and brutal

    d. It helped defend Europe from the Byzantine Empire

6. What impact did the feudal system have on the Crusades?

    a. It unified the Crusaders

    b. It helped gather volunteers

    c. It had no effect on the Crusades

    d. It led to infighting, causing more damage than good

Questions 7 - 9 refer to the following passage.

Passage 2 - Women and Advertising

Only in the last few generations have media messages been so widespread and so readily seen, heard, and read by so many people. Advertising is an important part of both selling and buying anything from soap to cereal to jeans. For whatever reason, more consumers are women than are men. Media message are subtle but powerful, and more attention has been paid lately to how these message affect women. Of all the products that women buy, makeup, clothes, and other stylistic or cosmetic products are among the most popular. This means that companies focus their advertising on women, promising them that their product will make her feel, look, or smell better than the next company's product will. This competition has resulted in advertising that is more and more ideal and less and less possible for everyday women. However, because women do look to these ideals and the products they represent as how they can potentially become, many women have developed unhealthy attitudes about themselves when they have failed to become those ideals.

In recent years, more companies have tried to change advertisements to be healthier for women. This includes featuring models of more sizes and addressing a huge outcry against unfair tools such as airbrushing and photo editing. There is debate about what the right balance between real and ideal is, because fashion is also considered art and some changes are made to purposefully elevate fashionable products and signify that they are creative, innovative, and the work of individual people. Artists want their freedom protected as much as women do, and advertising agencies are often caught in the middle.

Some claim that the companies who make these changes are not doing enough. Many people worry that there are still not enough models of different sizes and different ethnicities. Some people claim that companies use this healthier type of advertisement not for the good of women, but because they would like to sell products to the women who are looking for these kinds of messages. This is also a hard balance to find: companies do need to make money, and women do need to feel respected.

While the focus of this change has been on women, advertising can also affect men, and this change will hopefully be a lesson on media for all consumers.

7. The second paragraph states that advertising focuses on women

    a. to shape what the ideal should be

    b. because women buy makeup

    c. because women are easily persuaded

    d. because of the types of products that women buy

8. According to the passage, fashion artists and female consumers are at odds because

    a. there is a debate going on and disagreement drives people apart

    b. both of them are trying to protect their freedom to do something

    c. artists want to elevate their products above the reach of women

    d. women are creative, innovative, individual people

9. The author uses the phrase "for whatever reason" in this passage to

   a. keep the focus of the paragraph on media messages and not on the differences between men and women

   b. show that the reason for this is unimportant

   c. argue that it is stupid that more women are consumers than men

   d. show that he or she is tired of talking about why media messages are important

Questions 10 - 13 refer to the following email.

To: All Staff
From: John Smith (Managing Director)
Subject: Important Notice on Cleanliness

Dear Staff

I am quite pleased with the level of commitment and quality of work that you all have been putting in on late at your various duty posts. I have noticed that the last batches of staff training have really helped to improve our quality of service and we have indeed been getting lots of positive feedback from satisfied customers. However, I am forced to bring to your attention the issue of cleanliness, which from my position as Managing Director I have observed that we are scoring quite low in this regard.

As we should know, maintaining a clean work area does bring about several benefits. Here are some suggestions that I hope would improve the situation when put into practice.

- A swiffer duster or any other dusting tool should be kept in each office so that it can easily be used when it is noticed that dust has accumulated around the office.

- A trash can liner should be used along with the trash cans in each office to make it easier to empty the cans and replace the bags.

- A pack of sterilized wipes should be kept handy to be used to immediately address any liquid or coffee spills.

- The phone mouthpiece is a gathering point for germs and so it should be cleaned regularly.

I am aware that cleaning is the responsibility of the cleaning staff, but the nature of our business has made it plain that we cannot continue to leave the work place dirty until the cleaning crews resume at the end of work day. It is thus important that we all play our little roles to ensure that we maintain a sanitized and clean environment.

Thanking you all for your expected co-operation as usual.

John Smith
Managing Director
XXX Company
Houston, TX 69888

10. Who is responsible for cleaning in the office?

    a. All staff
    b. The cleaning staff
    c. No special person
    d. None of the above

11. Is the manager pleased with the quality of work overall?

    a. Yes
    b. No

12. What does he suggest for the trash cans?

    a. He has no special suggestion
    b. He suggest a duster
    c. He suggests a trash can liner
    d. None of the above.

13. When do the cleaning crew work?

    a. Once a week
    b. Twice a week
    c. Once a day
    d. None of the above

Reply to the Manager below - Questions 14 - 17

Dear Mr. Smith:

I read your recent email and I have a few suggestions. I think that you are suggesting that some of the ____14____ do the work of the ____15____.

I think that we should all be careful about cleanliness, however, I don't want my staff ____16____ of the cleaning staff. The staff in my office are quite busy already, and I don't want to give them ____17____ than they have.

Thank you,

Melissa Jones
Supervisor

14.

    a. Cleaning staff
    b. Office staff
    c. Managers
    d. None of the above

15.

    a. Cleaning staff
    b. Office staff
    c. Managers
    d. None of the above

16.

    a. Doing the job
    b. Talking to
    c. Working
    d. None of the above

17.

    a. Less work
    b. More work
    c. Some work
    d. None of the above

Questions 18 - 21 refer to the following email.

How to Study with a Twist!

There are countless different study habits and learning styles: some people spend hours in the library reading over notes, others create flashcards on their phone, others drink seven energy drinks and stay up all night. Some study habits are better (and healthier) than others, but in the end there are still a lot of options, and it can be hard to find the method that is right for you.

One common denominator between a lot of study advice, is that taking scheduled breaks can help keep your non-breaktime on track. Planning to take a break every 40 minutes, for 10 minutes, or for 20 minutes every hour, whatever works best for you, can help keep you focused in between. It gives you something to look forward to, and because your breaks are more frequent, you'll be less tempted to "accidentally" let them turn into an hour of procrastination.

But there is a way to take those breaks to the next level, both in terms of their usefulness and their fun (because why shouldn't studying be a bit of fun?).
Try making your breaks into dance breaks. Seriously. Set a timer if you need to, and every 40 minutes, take a 5 or 10 minute dance break! Put on a party jam, your favourite club song, or whatever makes you feel like moving your feet, and get up from your desk and dance around the room for 5 minutes. Shake your hair out, jump up and down, sing along even. Try to dance so hard you make yourself out of breath and get your heart pumping fast.

The dance break is an even greater strategy when you're studying with friends—if you can all have a 5 minute dance party and laugh together, your minds will be even sharper when you return to studying.

18. Does the author feel a dance break is for everyone?

    a. Yes, the author recommends it for everyone

    b. No, the author doesn't recommend it for everyone

19. What is a common study skills recommendation?

    a. Dance breaks are a common recommendation

    b. Taking breaks is a common recommendation

    c. Studying for long sessions is a common recommendation

    d. None of the above

20. What is one advantage of frequent breaks while studying?

    a. No particular advantage

    b. You will be less tempted to procrastinate

    c. Laughing with your friends

    d. None of the above

21. When does the author suggest a dance break is best?

    a. The author does not have any special time

    b. Every 40 minutes

    c. With friends

    d. None of the above

Response to this passage - Questions 22 - 25

I like ____22____ of this advice but can't agree with it all. Yes, I think taking breaks is ____23____ but what if you don't like dancing?

This essay is great if you like dancing or if you want to try dancing, but if you don't like dancing, So maybe if you want your essay to appeal to ____24____ you could have more suggestions on ____25____.

22.

    a. All

    b. Some

    c. None

23.

    a. Important

    b. Not important

    c. Somewhat important

    d. None of the above

24.

    a. Fewer people
    b. More people
    c. Students
    d. None of the above

25.

    a. How to dance
    b. Things to do on a break
    c. How to study
    d. None of the above

Questions 26 - 28 refer to the following table

Which School?

Oak St. English School

Immersion and conversation classes
Morning, Afternoon or Evening classes

Some teachers are native speakers

Private Lessons
Business English
Lessons for all ages

Prices from $35/hour to $75/hour

Fort St. English School

Convenient downtown location
Evening classes

All teachers are Native speakers

Private and Group lessons
IELTS Prep
Business English

Prices from $50 - $100

Hi Sandy - just looking at English schools as we talked about. I went through quite a few online and have found 2 schools.

I ___26___ the Fort St. English School. The seem more professional and I may want to take a few ___27___ to start. It is more expensive I know but I think it would really help to start. What were you thinking of?

It seems a little more ___28___ but I think it is worth it to have the convenient location.

26.

    a. Like

    b. Don't like

27.

    a. Group lessons

    b. Private Lessons

28.

    a. Better Qualified

    b. Cheaper

    c. Expensive

Questions 29 - 31 refer to the following passage

What Is Mardi Gras?

Mardi Gras is fast becoming one of the South's most famous and most celebrated holidays. The word Mardi Gras comes from the French and the literal translation is "Fat Tuesday." The holiday has also been called Shrove Tuesday, due to its associations with Lent. The purpose of Mardi Gras is to celebrate and enjoy before the Lenten season of fasting and repentance begins.
What originated by the French Explorers in New Orleans, Louisiana in the 17th century is now celebrated all over the world. Panama, Italy, Belgium and Brazil all host large scale Mardi Gras celebrations, and many smaller cities and towns celebrate this fun loving Tuesday as well. Usually held in February or early March, Mardi Gras is a day of extravagance, a day for people to eat, drink and be merry, to wear costumes, masks and to dance to jazz music.

The French explorers on the Mississippi River would be in shock today if they saw the opulence of the parades and floats that grace the New Orleans streets during Mardi Gras these days. Parades in New Orleans are divided by organizations. These are more commonly known as Krewes.

Being a member of a Krewe is quite a task because Krewes are responsible for overseeing the parades. Each Krewe's parade is ruled by a Mardi Gras "King and Queen." The role of the King and Queen is to "bestow" gifts on their adoring fans as the floats ride along the street. They throw doubloons, which is fake money and usually colored green, purple and gold, which are the colors of Mardi Gras. Beads in those color shades are also thrown and cups are thrown as well. Beads are by far the most popular souvenir of any Mardi Gras parade, with each spectator attempting to gather as many as possible.

29. The purpose of Mardi Gras is to

    a. Repent for a month.

    b. Celebrate in extravagant ways.

    c. Be a member of a Krewe.

    d. Explore the Mississippi.

30. Which group of people first began to hold Mardi Gras celebrations?

    a. Settlers from Italy

    b. Members of Krewes

    c. French explorers

    d. Belgium explorers

31. In the context of the passage, what does spectator mean?

    a. Someone who participates actively

    b. Someone who watches the parade's action

    c. Someone on one of the parade floats

    d. Someone who does not celebrate Mardi Gras

Questions 31 – 35 refer to the following passage.

Passage 1 - Who Was Anne Frank?

You may have heard mention of the word Holocaust in your History or English classes. The Holocaust took place from 1939-1945. It was an attempt by the Nazi party to purify the human race, by eliminating Jews, Gypsies, Catholics, homosexuals and others they deemed inferior to their "perfect" Aryan race. The Nazis used Concentration Camps, which were sometimes used as Death Camps, to exterminate the people they held in the camps. The saddest fact about the Holocaust was the over one million children under the age of sixteen died in a Nazi concentration camp. Just a few weeks before

World War II was over, Anne Frank was one of those children to die.

Before the Nazi party began its persecution of the Jews, Anne Frank had a happy live. She was born in June of 1929. In June of 1942, for her 13th birthday, she was given a simple present which would go onto impact the lives of millions of people around the world. That gift was a small red diary that she called Kitty. This diary was to become Anne's most treasured possession when she and her family hid from the Nazi's in a secret annex above her father's office building in Amsterdam.

For 25 months, Anne, her sister Margot, her parents, another family, and an elderly Jewish dentist hid from the Nazis in this tiny annex. They were never permitted to go outside and their food and supplies were brought to them by Miep Gies and her husband, who did not believe in the Nazi persecution of the Jews. It was a very difficult life for young Anne and she used Kitty as an outlet to describe her life in hiding. After 2 years, Anne and her family were betrayed and arrested by the Nazis. To this day, nobody is exactly sure who betrayed the Frank family and the other annex residents. Anne, her mother, and her sister were separated from Otto Frank, Anne's father. Then, Anne and Margot were separated from their mother. In March of 1945, Margot Frank died of starvation in a Concentration Camp. A few days later, at the age of 15, Anne Frank died of typhus. Of all the people who hid in the Annex, only Otto Frank survived the Holocaust.

Otto Frank returned to the Annex after World War II. It was there that he found Kitty, filled with Anne's thoughts and feelings about being a persecuted Jewish girl. Otto Frank had Anne's diary published in 1947 and it has remained continuously in print ever since. Today, the diary has been published in over 55 languages and more than 24 million copies have been sold around the world. The Diary of Anne Frank tells the story of a brave young woman who tried to see the good in all people.

32. From the context clues in the passage, what does the word Annex mean?

    a. Attic

    b. Bedroom

    c. Basement

    d. Kitchen

33. Why do you think Anne's diary has been published in 55 languages?

    a. So everyone could understand it.

    b. So people around the world could learn more about the horrors of the Holocaust.

    c. Because Anne was Jewish but hid in Amsterdam and died in Germany.

    d. Because Otto Frank spoke many languages.

34. From the description of Anne and Margot's deaths in the passage, what can we assume typhus is?

    a. The same as starving to death.

    b. An infection the Germans gave to Anne.

    c. A disease Anne caught in the concentration camp.

    d. Poison gas used by the Germans to kill Anne.

35. In the third paragraph, what does the word outlet mean?

    a. A place to plug things into the wall

    b. A store where Miep bought cheap supplies for the Frank family

    c. A hiding space similar to an Annex

    d. A place where Anne could express her private thoughts.

Answer Key

Part I - Listening

1. A
The tech is helping her connect her computer first

2. B
She has a wired connection

3. B
She can tell she has a wired connection because she has a thick blue wire at the back of her computer.

4. A
She didn't see the Control Panel because it was a different version

5. C
The tech told her to click on the Settings button because the control panel wasn't there

6. C
No, there weren't any networks

7. A
Yes her computer found an available network

8. C
To check if the connection was successful they opened a browser

9. A
Yahoo was her favourite website

10. B
He wanted her to drive because he needed a break.

11. C
The project at his work was not going well and the next few days were going to be very busy.

12. B
She had meetings all that day and all afternoon the next day

13. B
He was going to have to work Saturday and maybe Sunday

14. C
She wanted to do something fun on Sunday

15. B
Tom was going to school when he noticed the burning house.

16. B
Tom called the emergency services when he saw the house was on fire. From the passage, ". The teenager immediately called the emergency service and gave the address."

17. C
It took a long time for the fire department to arrive because the house was out of time

18. A
Most volcanoes are underwater

19. B
A split in the earth's plates causes volcanoes.

20. A
The volcano Vesuvius covered the city of Pompeii in minutes.

21. C
Shield volcanoes are common in the Hawaiian volcanic chain

22. B
Stratovolcanoes, which are tall conical mountains formed of lava flows

23. B
Underwater volcanoes do not have big explosions due to the weight of the water.

24. B
Mountains lions are found in Los Angeles backyards.

25. B
No, wild animals in urban areas is not new

26. B
People who are distracted easily have difficulty studying.

27. B
No the author does not believe in cramming.

28. B
The author is a distracted learner.

29. B
The author recommends making it into a game.

30. A
The author likes background music while studying.

Reading

1. A
The correct order of ingredients is brown sugar, baking soda, chocolate chips.

2. A
Disperse: to scatter in different directions or break up.

3. B
You can stop stirring the nuts when they are evenly distributed. From the passage, "Stir until the chocolate chips and nuts are evenly dispersed."

4. A
Choice B is incorrect; the author did not express their opinion on the subject matter. Choice C is incorrect, the author was not trying to prove a point, nor is the author trying to persuade.

5. C
Choice C is correct; historians believe it was brutal and bloody. Choice A is incorrect; there is no consensus that the Crusades achieved great things. Choice B is incorrect; it did not stabilize the Holy Lands. Choice D is incorrect, some his-

torians do believe this was the purpose but not all historians.

6. D
The feudal system led to infighting. Choice A is incorrect, it had the opposite effect. Choice B is incorrect, though this is a good answer, it is not the best answer. The Church asked for volunteers not the Feudal Lords. Choice C is incorrect, it did have an effect on the Crusades.

7. D
The other choices A, B, and C focus on portions of the second paragraph that are too narrow and do not relate to the specific portion of text in question. The complexity of the sentence may mislead students into selecting one of these answers, but rearranging or restating the sentence will lead the reader to the correct answer. In addition, choice A makes an assumption that may or may not be true about the intentions of the company, choice B focuses on one product rather than the idea of the products, and choice C makes an assumption about women that may or may not be true and is not supported by the text.

8. B
This question tests reader's attention to detail. If a reader selects A, he or she may have picked up on the use of the word "debate" and assumed, very logically, that the two are at odds because they are fighting; however, this is simply not supported in the text. Choice C also uses very specific quotes from the text, but it rearranges and gives them false meaning. The artists want to elevate their creations above the creations of other artists, thereby showing that they are "creative" and "innovative." Similarly, choice D takes phrases straight from the text and rearranges and confuses them. The artists are described as wanting to be "creative, innovative, individual people," not the women.

9. A
This phrase, used by the author, may seem flippant and dismissive if readers focus on the word "whatever" and misinterpret it as a popular, colloquial term. In this way, choices B and C may mislead the reader to selecting one of them by including the terms "unimportant" and "stupid," respectively. Choice D is a similar misreading, but doesn't make sense

when the phrase is at the beginning of the passage and the entire passage is on media messages. Choice A is literallyand contextually appropriate, and the reader can understand that the author would like to keep the introduction focused on the topic the passage is going to discuss.

10. B
Cleaning staff are responsible for cleaning - however the manager would like everyone to assist.

11. A
Yes the manager is pleased with the quality of work overall

12. C
He suggests a plastic liner for the trash cans

13. C
The cleaning crew comes in at the end of the work day.

14. B
Office staff. She is concerned the office staff will do the work of the cleaning staff.

15. A
Cleaning staff. She is concerned the office staff will do the work of the cleaning staff.

16. A
She doesn't want her staff **doing the job** of the cleaning staff.

17. B
She doesn't want her staff doing **more work.**

18. B
No the author does not recommend dance breaks for anyone.

19. B
Taking breaks when studying is a common recommendation.

20. B
One advantage of taking frequent breaks is you are less tempted to procrastinate.

21. B
The author suggests taking a break for 10 minutes every 40 minutes, or for 20 minutes every hour.

22. B
Some. The author like some of the advice but not all.

23. A
The author agrees taking breaks is important

24. B
The author doesn't like dancing so they suggest it could appeal to more people.

25. B
Since the author doesn't like dancing, she recommends suggestions on other things to do on a break.

26. A
She likes the Fort St. school.

27. B
She is thinking of private lessons to start.

28. C
The Fort St. school is more expensive.

29. B
The correct answer can be found in the fourth sentence of the first paragraph.

Choice A is incorrect because repenting begins the day AFTER Mardi Gras. Choice C is incorrect because you can celebrate Mardi Gras without being a member of a Krewe.

Choice D is incorrect because exploration does not play any role in a modern Mardi Gras celebration.

30. C
The first sentences of BOTH the 2nd and 3rd paragraphs mention that French explorers started this tradition in New Orleans.

Choices A, B and D are incorrect because they are just names of cities or countries listed in the 2nd paragraph.

31. B
In the final paragraph the word spectator is used to describe people who are watching the parade and catching cups, beads and doubloons.

Choices A and C are incorrect because we know the people who participate are part of Krewes. People who work the floats and parades are also part of Krewes

Choice D is incorrect because the passage makes no mention of people who do not celebrate Mardi Gras.

32. A
We know that an annex is like an attic because the text states the annex was above Otto Frank's building.

Choice B is incorrect because an office building doesn't have bedrooms. Choice C is incorrect because a basement would be below the office building. Choice D is incorrect because there would not be a kitchen in an office building.

33. B
The diary has been published in 55 languages so people all over the world can learn about Anne. That is why the passage says it has been continuously in print.

Choice A is incorrect because it is too vague. Choice C is incorrect because it was published after Anne died and she did not write in all three languages. Choice D is incorrect because the passage does not give us any information about what languages Otto Frank spoke.

34. C
Use the process of elimination to figure this out.

Choice A cannot be the correct answer because otherwise the passage would have simply said that Anne and Margot both died of starvation. Choices B and D cannot be correct because if the Germans had done something specifically to murder Anne, the passage would have stated that directly. By the process of elimination, choice C has to be the correct answer.

35. D

We can figure this out using context clues. The paragraph is talking about Anne's diary and so, outlet in this instance is a place where Anne can pour her feelings.

Choice A is incorrect answer. That is the literal meaning of the word outlet and the passage is using the figurative meaning. Choice B is incorrect because that is the secondary literal meaning of the word outlet, as in an outlet mall. Again, we are looking for figurative meaning. Choice C is incorrect because there are no clues in the text to support that answer.

How to Prepare for a Test

MOST STUDENTS HIDE THEIR HEADS AND PROCRASTINATE WHEN FACED WITH PREPARING FOR AN EXAM, HOPING THAT SOMEHOW THEY WILL BE SPARED THE AGONY, ESPECIALLY IF IT IS A BIG ONE THAT THEIR FUTURES RELY ON. Avoiding a test is what many students do best and unfortunately, they suffer the consequences because of their lack of preparation.

Test preparation requires strategy and dedication. It is the perfect training ground for a professional life. Besides having several reliable strategies, successful students also has a clear goal and know how to accomplish it. These tried and true concepts have worked well and will make your test preparation easier.

The Study Approach

Take responsibility for your own test preparation.

It is a common - but big - mistake to link your studying to someone else's. Study partners are great, but only if they are reliable. It is your job to be prepared for the test, even if a study partner fails you. Do not allow others to distract you from your goals.

Prioritize the time available to study

When do you learn best, early in the day or at night? Does your mind absorb and retain information most efficiently in small blocks of time, or do you require long stretches to get the most done? It is important to figure out the best blocks of time available to you when you can be the most productive. Try to consolidate activities to allow for longer periods of study time.

Find a quiet place where you will not be disturbed

Do not try to squeeze in quality study time in any old location. Find a quiet place with a minimum of distractions, such as the library, a park or even the laundry room. Good lighting is essential and you need to have comfortable seating and a desk surface large enough to hold your materials. It is probably not a great idea to study in your bedroom. You might be distracted by clothes on the floor, a book you have been planning to read, the telephone or something else. Besides, in the middle of studying, that bed will start to look very comfortable. Whatever you do, avoid using the bed as a place to study since you might fall asleep to avoiding studying!

The exception is flashcards. By far the most productive study time is sitting down and studying and studying only. However, with flashcards you can carry them with you and make use of odd moments, like standing in line or waiting for the bus. This isn't as productive, but it really helps and is definitely worth doing.

Determine what you need to study

Gather together your books, your notes, your laptop and any other materials needed to focus on your study for this exam. Ensure you have everything you need so you don't waste time. Remember paper, pencils and erasers, sticky notes, bottled water and a snack. Keep your phone with you if you need it to find essential information, but keep it turned off so others can't distract you.

Have a positive attitude

It is essential that you approach your studies for the test with an attitude that says you will pass it. And pass it with flying colors! This is one of the most important keys to successful studying. Believing that you are capable helps you to become capable.

The Strategy of Studying

Review class notes

Stay on top of class notes and assignments by reviewing them frequently and regularly and regularly. Re-writing notes can be a terrific study trick, as it helps lock in information. Pay special attention to any comments that have been made by the teacher. If a study guide has been made available as part of the class materials, use it! It will be a valuable tool to use for studying.

Estimate how much time you will need

If you are concerned about the amount of time you have available it is a good idea to set up a schedule so that you do not get bogged down on one section and end without enough time left to study other things. Remember to schedule break time, and use that time for a little exercise or other stress reducing techniques.

Test yourself to determine your weaknesses

Look online for additional assessment and evaluation tools available like practice questions for a particular subject. Visit our website https://www.test-preparation.ca for test tips and more practice questions. Once you have determined your weaknesses, you can focus on these, and just brush up on the other areas of the exam.

Mental Prep – How to Psych Yourself Up for a Test

Since tests are often a big factor in your final grade or acceptance into a program, it is understandable that taking tests can create a great deal of anxiety for many students. Even students who know they have learned the required material find their minds going blank as they stare at the test booklet. You can avoid test anxiety by preparing yourself mentally. One easy way to overcome that anxiety is to prepare mentally for the test with a few simple techniques. **Do not procrastinate**

Study the material for the test when it becomes available, and continue to review the material until the test day. By waiting until the last minute and trying to cram for the test the night before, you actually increase anxiety. This leads to negative self-talk, which becomes self-fulfilling. Telling yourself "I can't learn this. I am going to fail" is a pretty sure indication that you are right.

Positive self-talk.

Positive self-talk drowns out negative self-talk and to increases your confidence level. Whenever you begin feeling overwhelmed or anxious about the test, remind yourself that you have studied enough, you know the material and that you will pass the test. Both negative and positive self-talk are really just your fantasy, so why not choose to be a winner?

Do not compare yourself to others.

Do not compare yourself to other students. Instead, focus on your strengths and weaknesses and prepare accordingly. Regardless of how others perform, your performance is the only one that matters to your grade. Comparing yourself to others increases your anxiety and negative self-talk before the test.

Visualize.

Make a mental image of yourself taking the test. You know the answers and feel relaxed. Visualize doing well on the test and having no problems with the material. Visualizations can increase your confidence and decrease the anxiety you might otherwise feel before the test. Instead of thinking of this as a test, see it as an opportunity to demonstrate what you have learned!

How to Take a Test

EVERYONE KNOWS THAT TAKING AN EXAM IS STRESSFUL, BUT IT DOES NOT HAVE TO BE THAT BAD! There are a few simple things that you can do to increase your score on any type of test. Take a look at these tips and consider how you can incorporate them into your study time.

OK - so you are in the test room - Here is what to do!

Reading the Instructions

This is the most basic point, but one that, surprisingly, many students ignore and it costs big time! Since reading the instructions is one of the most common, and 100% preventable mistakes, we have a whole section just on reading instructions.

Pay close attention to the sample questions. Almost all standardized tests offer sample questions, paired with their correct solutions. Go through these to make sure that you understand what they mean and how they arrived at the correct answer. Do not be afraid to ask the test supervisor for help with a sample that confuses you, or instructions that you are unsure of.

Tips for Reading the Question

We could write pages and pages of tips just on reading the test questions. Here are a few that will help you the most.

- **Think first.** Before you look at the answer, read and think about the question. It is best to try to come up with the correct answer before you look at the options. This way, when the test-writer tries to trick you with a close answer, you will not fall for it.

- **Make it true or false.** If a question confuses you, then look at each answer option and think of it as a "true" "false" question. Select the one that seems most likely to be "true."

- **Mark the Question.** Don't be afraid to mark up the test booklet. Unless you are specifically told not to mark in the booklet, use it to your advantage.

- **Circle Key Words.** As you are reading the question, underline or circle key words. This helps you to focus on the most critical information needed to solve the problem. For example, if the question said, "Which of these is not a synonym for huge?" You might circle "not," "synonym" and "huge." That clears away the clutter and lets you focus on what is important.

- **Always underline these words:** all, none, always, never, most, best, true, false and except.

- **Eliminate.** Elimination is the best strategy for multiple choice answers *and* questions. If you are confused by lengthy questions, cross out anything that you think is irrelevant, obviously wrong, or information that you think is offered to distract you. Elimination is the most valuable strategy!

- **Do not try to read between the lines.** Usually, questions are written to be straightforward, with no deep, underlying meaning. Generally, the simple answer really is the correct answer. Do not over-analyze!

How to Take a Test - The Basics

Some sections of the test are designed to assess your ability to quickly grab the necessary information; this type of exam makes speed a priority. Others are more concerned with your depth of knowledge, and how accurate it is. When you start a new section of the test, look it over to determine whether the test is for speed or accuracy. If the test is for speed (a lot of questions and a short time), your strategy is clear; answer as many questions as quickly as possible.

The CAEL® does NOT penalize for wrong answers, so if all else fails, guess and make sure you answer every question.

Make time your friend

Budget your time from the beginning until you are finished, and stick to it! The time for each section will be included in the instructions.

Easy does it

One smart way to tackle a test is to locate the easy questions and answer those first. This is a time-tested strategy that never fails, because it saves you a lot of unnecessary anxiety. First, read the question and decide if you can answer it in less than a minute. If so, complete the question and go to the next one. If not, skip it for now and continue to the next question. By the time you have completed the first pass through this section of the exam, you will have answered a good number of questions. Not only does it boost your confidence, relieve anxiety and kick your memory up a notch, you will know exactly how many questions remain and can allot the rest of your time accordingly. Think of doing the easy questions first as a warm-up!

Do not watch your watch

At best, taking an important exam is an uncomfortable situation. If you are like most people, you might be tempted to subconsciously distract yourself from the task at hand. One of the most common ways is by becoming obsessed with your watch or the wall clock. Do not watch your watch! Take it off and place it on the top corner of your desk, far enough away that you will not be tempted to look at it every two minutes. Better still, turn the watch face away from you. That way, every time you try to sneak a peek, you will be reminded to refocus your attention to the task at hand. Give yourself permission to check your watch or the wall clock after you complete each section. Focus on answering the questions, not on how many minutes have elapsed since you last looked at it.

Divide and conquer

What should you do when you come across a question that is so complicated you may not even be certain what is being asked? As we have suggested, the first time through, skip the question. At some point, you will need to return to it and get it under control. The best way to handle questions that leave you feeling so anxious you can hardly think is by breaking them into manageable pieces. Solving smaller bits is always easier. For complicated questions, divide them into bite-sized pieces and solve these smaller sets separately. Once you understand what the reduced sections are really saying, it will be much easier to put them together and get a handle on the bigger question. This may not work with every question - see below for how to deal with questions you cannot break down.

Reason your way through the toughest questions

If you find that a question is so dense you can't figure out how to break it into smaller pieces, there are a few strategies that might help. First, read the question again and look for hints. Can you re-word the question in one or more different ways? This may give you clues. Look for words that can function as either verbs or nouns, and try to figure out what the questions is asking from the sentence structure. Remember that many nouns in English have several different meanings. While some of those meanings might be related, sometimes they are completely distinct. If reading the sentence one way does not make sense, consider a different definition or meaning for a key word.

The truth is, it is not always necessary to understand a question to arrive at a correct answer! The most successful strategy for multiple choice is Elimination. Frequently, at least one answer is clearly wrong and can be crossed off the list of possible correct answers. Next, look at the remaining answers and eliminate any that are only partially true. You may still have to flat-out guess from time to time, but using the process of elimination will help you make your way to the correct answer more often than not - even when you don't know what the question means!

Do not leave early

Use all the time allotted to you, even if you can't wait to get out of the testing room. Instead, once you have finished, spend the remaining time reviewing your answers. Go back to those questions that were most difficult for you and review your response. Another good way to use this time is to return to multiple-choice questions in which you filled in a bubble. Do a spot check, reviewing every fifth or sixth question to make sure your answer coincides with the bubble you filled in. This is a great way to catch yourself if you made a mistake, skipped a bubble and therefore put all your answers in the wrong bubbles!

Become a super sleuth and look for careless errors. Look for questions that have double negatives or other odd phrasing; they might be an attempt to throw you off. Careless errors on your part might be the result of skimming a question and missing a key word. Words such as "always," "never," "sometimes," "rarely" and the like can give a strong indication of the answer the question is really seeking. Don't throw away points by being careless!

Just as you budgeted time at the beginning of the test to allow for easy and more difficult questions, be sure to budget sufficient time to review your answers. On essay questions and math questions where you are required to show your work, check your writing to make sure it is legible.

Math questions can be especially tricky. The best way to double check math questions is by figuring the answer using a different method, if possible.

Here is another terrific tip. It is likely that no matter how hard you try, you will have a handful of questions you just are not sure of. Keep them in mind as you read through the rest of the test. If you can't answer a question, looking back over the test to find a different question that addresses the same topic might give you clues.

We know that taking the test has been stressful and you can hardly wait to escape. Just Leaving before you double-check as much as possible can be a quick trip to disaster. Taking a few extra minutes can make the difference between getting a bad grade and a great one. Besides, there will be lots of time to relax and celebrate after the test is turned in.

In the Test Room – What you MUST do!

If you are like the rest of the world, there is almost nothing you would rather avoid than taking a test. Unfortunately, that is not an option if you want to pass. Rather than suffer, consider a few attitude adjustments that might turn the experience from a horrible one to...well, an interesting one! Take a look at these tips. Simply changing how you perceive the experience can change the experience itself.

You have to take the test - you can't change that. What you can change, and the only thing that you can change, is your attitude -so get a grip - you can do it!

Get in the mood

After weeks of studying, the big day has finally arrived. The worst thing you can do to yourself is arrive at the test site feeling frustrated, worried, and anxious. Keep a check on your emotional state. If your emotions are shaky before a test it can determine how well you do on the test. It is extremely important that you pump yourself up, believe in yourself, and use that confidence to get in the mood!

Don't fight reality

Students often resent tests, and with good reason. After all, many people do not test well, and they know the grade they end with does not accurately reflect their true knowledge. It is easy to feel resentful because tests classify students and create categories that just don't seem fair. Face it: Students who are great at rote memorization and not that good at actually analyzing material often score higher than those who might be more creative thinkers and balk at simply memorizing cold, hard facts. It may not be fair, but there it is anyway. Conformity is an asset on tests, and creativity is often a liability. There is no point in wasting time or energy being upset about this reality. Your first step is to accept the reality and get used to it. You will get higher marks when you realize tests do count and that you must give them your best effort. Think about your future and the career that is easier to achieve if you have consistently earned high grades. Avoid negative energy and focus on anything that lifts your enthusiasm and increases your motivation.

Get there early enough to relax

If you are wound up, tense, scared, anxious, or feeling rushed, it will cost you. Get to the exam room early and relax before you go in. This way, when the exam starts, you are comfortable and ready to apply yourself. Of course, you do not want to arrive so early that you are the only one there. That will not help you relax; it will only give you too much time to sit there, worry and get wound up all over again.

If you can, visit the room where you will be taking your exam a few days ahead of time. Having a visual image of the room can be surprisingly calming, because it takes away one of the big 'unknowns'. Not only that, but once you have visited, you know how to get there and will not be worried about getting lost. Furthermore, driving to the test site once lets you know how much time you need to allow for the trip. That means three potential stressors have been eliminated all at once.

Get it down on paper

One advantage of arriving early is that it allows you time to recreate notes. If you spend a lot of time worrying about whether you will be able to remember information like names, dates, places, and mathematical formulas, there is a solution for that. Unless the exam you are taking allows you to use your books and notes, (and very few do) you will have to rely on memory. Arriving early gives to time to tap into your memory and jot down key pieces of information you know that will be asked. Just make certain you are allowed to make notes once you are in the testing site; not all locations will permit it. Once you get your test, on a small piece of paper write down everything you are afraid you will forget. It will take a minute or two but by dumping your worries onto the page you have effectively eliminated a certain amount of anxiety and driven off the panic you feel.

Get comfortable in your chair

Here is a clever technique that releases physical stress and helps you get comfortable, even relaxed in your body. You will tense and hold each of your muscles for just a few seconds. The trick is, you must tense them hard for the technique to work. You might want to practice this technique a few times at home; you do not want an unfamiliar technique to add to your stress just before a test, after all! Once you are at the test site, this exercise can always be done in the rest room or another quiet location.

Start with the muscles in your face then work down your body. Tense, squeeze and hold the muscles for a moment or two. Notice the feel of every muscle as you go down your body. Scowl to tense your forehead, pull in your chin to tense your neck. Squeeze your shoulders down to tense your back. Pull in your stomach all the way back to your ribs, make your lower back tight then stretch your fingers. Tense your leg muscles and calves then stretch your feet and your toes. You should be as stiff as a board throughout your entire body.

Now relax your muscles in reverse starting with your toes.

Notice how all the muscles feel as you relax them one by one. Once you have released a muscle or set of muscles, allow them to remain relaxed as you proceed up your body. Focus on how you are feeling as all the tension leaves. Start breathing deeply when you get to your chest muscles. By the time you have found your chair, you will be so relaxed it will feel like bliss!

Fight distraction

A lucky few are able to focus deeply when taking an important examination, but most people are easily distracted, probably because they would rather be any place else! There are several things you can do to protect yourself from distraction.

Stay away from windows.

If you sit near a window you are adding an unnecessary distraction.

Choose a seat away from the aisle so you do not become distracted by people who leave early. People who leave the exam room early are often the ones who fail. Do not compare your time to theirs.

Of course, you love your friends; that's why they are your friends! In the test room, however, they should become complete strangers inside your mind. Forget they are there. The first step is to physically distance yourself from friends or classmates. That way, you will not be tempted to glance at them to see how they are doing, and there will be no chance of eye contact that could either distract you or even lead to an accusation of cheating. Furthermore, if they are feeling stressed because they did not spend the focused time studying that you did, their anxiety is less likely to permeate your hard-earned calm.

Of course, you will want to choose a seat where there is sufficient light. Nothing is worse than trying to take an important examination under flickering lights or dim bulbs.

Ask the instructor or exam proctor to close the door if there is a lot of noise outside. If the instructor or proctor is unable to do so, block out the noise as best you can. Do not let anything disturb you.

The CAEL® does not allow any personal items in the exam room. Eat protein, complex carbohydrates and a little fat to keep you feeling full and to supercharge your energy. Nothing is worse than a sudden drop in blood sugar during an exam.

Do not allow yourself to become distracted by being too cold or hot. Regardless of the weather outside, carry a sweater, scarf or jacket if the air conditioning at the test site is set too high, or the heat set too low. By the same token, dress in layers so that you are prepared for a range of temperatures.

Watch Caffeine

Drinking a gallon of coffee or gulping a few energy drinks might seem like a great idea, but it is, in fact, a very bad one. Caffeine, pep pills or other artificial sources of energy are more likely to leave you feeling rushed and ragged. Your brain might be clicking along, all right, but chances are good it is not clicking along on the right track! Furthermore, drinking coffee or energy drinks will mean frequent trips to the rest room. This will cut into the time you should be spending answering questions and is a distraction in itself, since each time you need to leave the room you lose focus. Pep pills will only make it harder for you to think straight when solving complicated problems.

At the same time, if anxiety is your problem try to find ways around using tranquilizers during test-taking time. Even medically prescribed anti-anxiety medication can make you less alert and even decrease your motivation. Being motivated is what you need to get you through an exam. If your anxiety is so bad that it threatens to interfere with your ability to take an exam, speak to your doctor and ask for documentation. Many testing sites will allow non-distracting test rooms, extended testing time and other accommodations with a doctor's note that explains the situation is made available.

Keep Breathing

It might not make a lot of sense, but when people become anxious, tense, or scared, their breathing becomes shallow and, sometimes stop breathing all together! Pay attention to your emotions, and when you are feeling worried, focus on your breathing. Take a moment to remind yourself to breathe deeply and regularly. Drawing in steady, deep breaths energizes the body. When you continue to breathe deeply you will notice you exhale all the tension.

If you feel you need to, try rehearsing breathing at home. With continued practice of this relaxation technique, you will begin to know the muscles that tense up under pressure. Call these your "signal muscles." These are the ones that will speak to you first, begging you to relax. Take the time to listen to those muscles and do as they ask. With just a little breathing practice, you will get into the habit of checking yourself regularly and when you realize you are tense, relaxation will become second nature.

Avoid Anxiety Before a Test

Manage your time effectively

This is a key to your success! You need blocks of uninterrupted time to study all the pertinent material. Creating and maintaining a schedule will help keep you on track, and will remind family members and friends that you are not available. Under no circumstances should you change your blocks of study time to accommodate someone else, or cancel a study session to do something more fun. Do not interfere with your study time for any reason!

Relax

Use whatever works best for you to relieve stress. Some folks like a good, calming stretch with yoga, others find expressing themselves through journaling to be useful. Some hit the floor for a series of crunches or planks, and still others take a slow stroll around the garden. Integrate a little relaxation time into your schedule, and treat that time, too, as sacred.

Eat healthy

Instead of reaching for the chips and chocolate, fresh fruits and vegetables are not only yummy but offer nutritional benefits that help to relieve stress. Some foods accelerate stress instead of reducing it and should be avoided. Foods that add to higher anxiety include artificial sweeteners, candy and other sugary foods, carbonated sodas, chips, chocolate, eggs, fried foods, junk foods, processed foods, red meat, and other foods containing preservatives or heavy spices. Instead, eat a bowl of berries and some yogurt!

Get plenty of ZZZZZZZs

Do not cram or try to do an all-nighter. If you created a study schedule at the beginning, and if you have stuck with that schedule, have confidence! Staying up too late trying to cram in last-minute bits of information is going to leave you exhausted the next day. Besides, whatever new information you cram in will only displace all the important ideas you've spent weeks learning. Remember: You need to be alert and fully functional the day of the exam

Have confidence in yourself!

Everyone experiences some anxiety when taking a test, but exhibiting a positive attitude banishes anxiety and fills you with the knowledge you really do know what you need to know. This is your opportunity to show how well prepared you are. Go for it!

Do not chitchat with friends

Let your friends know ahead of time that it is not anything

personal, but you are going to ignore them in the test room! You need to find a seat away from doors and windows, one that has good lighting, and get comfortable. If other students are worried their anxiety could be detrimental to you; of course, you do not have to tell your friends that. If you are afraid they will be offended, tell them you are protecting them from your anxiety!

Common Test-Taking Mistakes

Taking a test is not much fun at best. When you take a test and make a stupid mistake that negatively affects your grade, it is natural to be very upset, especially when it is something that could have been easily avoided. So what are some of the common mistakes that are made on tests?

Put your name on the test!

How could you possibly forget to put your name on a test? You would be amazed at how often that happens. Very often, tests without names are thrown out immediately, resulting in a failing grade.

Marking the wrong multiple-choice answer

It is important to work at a steady pace, but that does not mean bolting through the questions. Be sure the answer you are marking is the one you mean to. If the bubble you need to fill in or the answer you need to circle is 'C', do not allow yourself to get distracted and select 'B' instead.

Answering a question twice

Some multiple-choice test questions have two very similar answers. If you are in too much of a hurry, you might select them both. Remember that only one answer is correct, so if you choose more than one, you have automatically failed that question.

Mishandling a difficult question

We recommend skipping difficult questions and returning to them later, but beware! First, be certain that you do return to the question. Circling the entire passage or placing a large question mark beside it will help you spot it when you are reviewing your test. Secondly, if you are not careful to skip the question, you can mess yourself up badly. Imagine that a question is too difficult and you decide to save it for later. You read the next question, which you know the answer to, and you fill in that answer. You continue to the end of the test then return to the difficult question only to discover you didn't actually skip it! Instead, you inserted the answer to the following question in the spot reserved for the harder one, thus throwing off the remainder of your test!

Incorrectly Transferring an answer from scratch paper

This can happen easily if you are trying to hurry! Double check any answer you have figured out on scratch paper, and make sure what you have written on the test itself is an exact match!

Thinking too much

Generally, your first thought is your best thought. If you worry yourself into insecurity, your self-doubts can trick you into choosing an incorrect answer when your first impulse was the right one!

Conclusion

CONGRATULATIONS! You have made it this far because you have applied yourself diligently to practicing for the exam and no doubt improved your potential score considerably! Getting into a good school is a huge step in a journey that might be challenging at times but will be many times more rewarding and fulfilling. That is why being prepared is so important.

Good Luck!

Register for Free Updates and More Practice Test Questions

Register your purchase at https://www.test-preparation.ca/register/

for updates, free test tips and more practice test questions.

Online Resources

How to Prepare for a Test - The Ultimate Guide

https://www.test-preparation.ca/prepare-test/

Learning Styles - The Complete Guide

https://www.test-preparation.ca/learning-style/

Test Anxiety Secrets!

https://www.test-preparation.ca/test-anxiety/

Time Management on a Test

https://www.test-preparation.ca/time-management/

Flash Cards - The Complete Guide

https://www.test-preparation.ca/flash-cards/

Test Preparation Video Series

https://www.test-preparation.ca/test-video/

How to Memorize - The Complete Guide

https://www.test-preparation.ca/memorize/

www.ingramcontent.com/pod-product-compliance
Lightning Source LLC
Chambersburg PA
CBHW072014070526
44583CB00015B/1482